About Reveille

"Reveille has the elegance of a fine lady. I have also witnessed this lady when she has been challenged. She always answers the call to action with a spirited response. Her never-say-die attitude, whether the score is hopelessly out of reach or not, represents the true spirit of Aggieland." —MARK THURMOND, former A&M All-American pitcher and 1984 World Series Game 1 starter

"Direct, honest, and open, the collie is unique in not only the dog world, but in our world as well. . . . having worked with three generations of the world's greatest collies, Lassie VII, Lassie VIII, and Lassie IX, this Baylor grad will always be a bit jealous that A&M has a collie and we don't." —ACE COLLINS, Lassie biographer

"Believe me, I know the power and magic of a collie. A collie changed my life. For as long as I live, I will be proud of my partnership with Lassie and I'll always hold the breed dear to my heart. My mom was from the great state of Texas, and it's always been a special place to me for that reason. Now it's special for two reasons: Mom and Reveille. All that's missing is apple pie!" —JON PROVOST, actor and the original Timmy from the Lassie series

"Reveille was always a 'gamer.' She was pretty laid back when you would see her on campus, but on game day she had an increased intensity. I'd see her sometimes on the sidelines during a game, and she'd be barking out instructions. I'm not positive, but I think her instructions were always to give her the ball. In that regard, she was a lot like some of the running backs I've played with." —DAT NGUYEN, NFL linebacker and former A&M All-American

"I was out of here in '67, and in 2002—twenty-five years later—I got my first chance to scratch Reveille behind the ears. I think every student ought to get that chance. And they ought to take the dog over to the MSC and line the students up to pet her. The ones that she growls at, snarls at, or bites should be kicked out of school right then, because they are obviously not cut out to be Aggies if Rev doesn't like them." —NEAL BOORTZ, nationally syndicated talk show host

"The type of animal that she is—friendly, warm, loyal, but still with a statuesque, prideful appearance—kind of represents what Texas A&M and its students are all about." —DENNIS FRANCHIONE, Texas A&M head football coach

"It's not just her face that is the identity. Instead, it is her heart. . . . Reveille has also been quite a trendsetter for all females on the Texas A&M campus." —CARRI BAKER-WELLS, first female president of the 12th Man Foundation

"As a television executive, I can assure you that she is great for the cameras." —JON HEIDTKE, general manager of FOX Sports Net

"Unlike the mascots of many universities, ours is not a refugee from some zoo seen only on game day, but a living, breathing presence seen all over campus all the time. Reveille is a part of A&M's daily life, including in the classroom." —DR. ROBERT M. GATES, Texas A&M University president

"Thousands of beautiful women have come and gone through Texas A&M since the campus was first opened to women. But I just have one thing to say to all the young women who are considering attending A&M: No matter how stunning you may be, you will always take a back seat to Reveille in a beauty contest." —KANDACE KRUEGER, 2001 Miss USA

"I love Texas A&M. I love dogs. And I love things that enhance the atmosphere of college athletics. So, you can see that Reveille would rank pretty high on my list of favorites, because she represents all of those things." —SHELBY METCALF, former A&M basketball coach

"Rev enjoyed being the center of attention. My girlfriend at the time is now my wife, Stephanie. . . . when I gave attention to Stephanie, Rev just kind of turned up her nose. . . . Rev liked all the attention to herself, and in a lot of cases, that's the way it was." —JEFF BAILEY, Mascot Corporal in 1997–98

"I went to Yale. There, a bulldog was the mascot, but somehow, the jowled bulldog's status got diminished over the years, while Reveille lives on, sparking the Aggies on to greatness. Go Reveille." —GEORGE H. W. BUSH, former president of the United States

Reveille

NUMBER 100

Centennial Series of the Association of Former Students,

Texas A&M University

Reveille

FIRST LADY OF TEXAS A&M

Rusty Burson & Vannessa Burson '91

TEXAS A&M UNIVERSITY PRESS • COLLEGE STATION

LIBRARY OF CONGRESS CATALOGING-IN-PUBLICATION DATA

Burson, Rusty.
    Reveille : First Lady of Texas A&M / Rusty Burson and Vannessa Burson.—1st ed.
        p.   cm.—(Centennial series of the Association of Former Students, Texas A&M
University ; no. 100)
    Includes index.
    ISBN 1-58544-348-4 (cloth : alk. paper)
    1. Texas A&M University—Mascots—History.   2. Texas A&M Aggies (Football
team)—History.   I. Burson, Vannessa.   II. Title.   III. Series.
    GV958.T44B87   2004
    378.764'242—dc22   2004002543

To our parents,

Vicki Pekurney, Russ Burson, Rodonnah Briscoe,

and the late Melvin Blasingame,

for raising us with a sincere appreciation for wet noses,

wagging tails, and the pitter patter of paws.

And to our own canine "girls,"

who have helped to make our house a home:

Shelby (1988–97)

Harley (1992–2000)

Becky & Bonnie

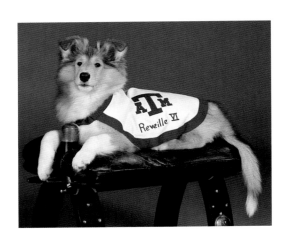

Contents

Preface

No matter how many times it happened, former Reveille handler Bo Wilson never ceased to be amazed. He was holding Reveille's leash, but considering the number of smiles, laughs, and Kodak moments he was treated to in one year, he could just as easily have been holding Santa's reins. With Reveille at his side, Wilson watched youngsters at children's hospitals forget their fears and ailments; he witnessed the faces of elderly men and women light up like children; and he watched as people of all walks of life touched a dog not just with their hands, but also with their hearts.

"Probably the most amazing thing about being the Mascot Corporal was just seeing how many people Reveille touches and what kind of impact she has on them," said Wilson, Texas A&M's mascot handler in 2000–2001. "It was always amazing to see the power and pull she has on people of all ages. Whether it's because she is a symbol of A&M, a celebrity, or just because she is a dog, she has remarkable reach."

She reached us a long time ago. Even as I grew up as a huge Baylor fan (my dad is a Baylor graduate), I was always drawn to Reveille. I once despised Texas A&M's football team, but I was always captivated by the canine on the sideline. Though I rooted against the Aggies, I figured there must be something awfully special about a university that treated a dog with such honor, respect, and love. I was right. When I fell in love with Texas A&M later in life, I became even more impressed with the tradition of Reveille. And when I fell in love with one Aggie, in particular, we became a family of Reveille fans. Reveille dolls line our kids' rooms. Our son never needed a security blanket; instead he clung to a faded, love-worn Reveille doll. Our daughter doesn't own a piggy bank; she's stuffing coins into a ceramic Rev.

That's why we loved the thought of doing this book. Although only one of us actually graduated from Texas A&M (Vannessa is class of 1991), we both love what Texas A&M represents. And of all the traditions we admire at A&M, Reveille has always topped the list. What can we say? We're dog people, and this book is for and about dog people—people who are willing to go to whatever lengths necessary to experience the blessings of being loved by a dog.

We have always believed the Reveille tradition is one of the most compelling in the collegiate mascot domain because of the way she wound up on this campus and then stole the hearts of the cadets who found her. Other schools have canine mascots, and many universities have some sort of live mascot. In terms of their origins, sentimental value, and role on campus, Aggies don't believe any of them can carry Reveille's water bowl.

Writing this book has been a labor of love for us. It created plenty of long days and sleepless nights, but it also increased our belief in the unique qualities of Texas A&M. This university is a special place, and the Reveille tradition is one we cherish. The book has introduced us to some remarkable men and women— fellow dog people who also believe that a house really isn't a home until it features backyard holes and teeth marks on the baseboards. It brought us into close contact with Reveille VII, and to the delight of our children, it also brought her into our home on several occasions. It also brought us closer to our own dogs,

making us appreciate them more and value the short time they spend in our lives. During the writing of this book, we also attended, as a family, the funeral of Reveille VI, which spawned the question from our children: Do dogs go to heaven?

Our deeply philosophical answer: "We're really not sure." But as we told our kids, we're certain that dogs are a gift from God. Until we make it to heaven to see for ourselves, they may be the best example of unconditional love on this side of the Pearly Gates. We obviously believe dogs are special, and we believe the story of Reveille exemplifies not only the instinctive and distinctive qualities of canines, but also the blessings and benefits that come to those who call themselves "dog people."

Texas A&M is filled with those kinds of people— people who are cheerfully committed to protecting, preserving, and promoting the legacy of a stray pup that wandered onto campus and into Aggie lore. Mahatma Gandhi once said that "the great test of a nation and its moral progress can be judged by the way its animals are treated." Perhaps the same applies to a university.

Did you know:

- The pink granite block T that bears the Reveille name was originally erected on April 21, 1947. The memorial, which once was placed along the outer wall of the old horseshoe in the north end zone, is now inside the stadium on the front rows of the lower-level end zone seats on the north end.

- Prior to being named "Reveille," the original, black pup that etched its place in A&M history was nicknamed "Home Brew."

- Reveille VII's registered name with the American Kennel Club is "Argent Barksdale Reveille 7," known to those closest to her as "Rev Sev." Reveille VII's uncle, "Champion Argent Big Bang" (also known as "Bam Bam"), was the AKC Best of Breed in 2001.

- Reveille V once won an overall "Best Legs" contest on campus that was sponsored by the United Way. Two human entries won the best legs for women and the best legs for men.

- It takes at least a full hour to wash and blow dry Reveille's thick, sable coat.

- A human mascot dressed as Ol' Sarge was introduced to Aggieland in 1987. The concept was largely unaccepted and quite unpopular with most of the fans.

- Not only was Rev I a general in the K-9 unit of WAGS, but she was one of only twenty-four members in the United States of the American Red Cross Dog Chapter.

- When Reveille appears in public wearing her blanket, her handler must also be in full uniform, complete with a tie.

- Reveille II, who made a name for herself as the "naughty girl of Aggieland," was known for her spunk, zeal, and biting rival coaches and referees who made calls she did not like. Interestingly, it is said that she never bit anyone when the Aggies were in the lead.

- H. S. Dan Boone, '46, who planned the funeral for Reveille I, bought her casket from Hillier Funeral Home for fifteen dollars. He also handled the funds that were used to pay Miss Marie Haynes, the artist commissioned to paint a portrait of Reveille I. The working sketch for the painting was given to Mr. Boone by Miss Haynes. He considered it his prize possession and later gave it to his brother, future Industrial Engineering Department head James L. Boone, '44, as a wedding gift.

- Reveille accompanied Texas A&M University President Robert M. Gates as he visited the 2003 recipients of the Distinguished Alumnus award to inform them they had been selected.

Reveille

CHAPTER 1

Puppy Breath

BIRTH OF A TRADITION

A SURGICAL TEAM of sixteen gathered inside the Fort Lauderdale, Florida, hospital on the morning of October 9, 2000, hoping—even praying—for the best. All of the preliminary tests during the mother's pregnancy had been positive up to that point, producing an optimistic outlook inside the operating room. In fact, a diagnostic ultrasound all the way back on day 26 of the pregnancy revealed a strong little heart beating rhythmically on the monitor. Even the mother's name, "Hope," seemed to be a precursor of a positive procedure. Under normal circumstances, this renowned medical team would hardly bat an eye at the routine nature of this particular Cesarean section.

This was not, however, a typical delivery day. The beating heart inside Hope's womb could possibly be the heir to a throne of sorts, symbolically representing a passionate throng of roughly a quarter-million sub-jects. But it all depended upon the newborn's sex, and unlike the traditional royal scenario, an army of maroon-blooded men and women waited in buoyant expectation of only a female. A male—no matter how healthy, strong, or cute—would simply not suffice in this particular situation. A momentary hush fell over the operating room as the wet and wiggling ball of life was lifted through the surgical incision along Hope's abdomen. Instantly, the possible heir was whisked away by a neurologist—even prior to its sex being determined—to clear the airways and perform a quick once-over. "We still didn't even know what the sex was," said Dr. Cindi Bossart, perhaps the most interested and animated observer inside the operating room. "Then finally, the neurologist returned and pronounced her normal, healthy, and 100 percent female. We had our little girl."

Bound for Bryan–College Station, Reveille VII takes the university plane from her birthplace in Florida with, among others, former Texas A&M president Ray Bowen (back left). Courtesy Bo Wilson

Technically speaking, they had the sable, bitch, American collie puppy that would inherit the title as Reveille VII and assume her reign in College Station, Texas. But please, in the name of Sul Ross, James Earl Rudder, Edwin Jackson Kyle, and every other respected figure in the history of Texas A&M University, choose your words carefully when referencing "Rev." Veterinary terms—no matter how clinically correct—simply do not seem appropriate for the revered mascot of one of the nation's largest and most spirited universities. In Aggieland, at least, Reveille is to the doggie domain what Lady Diana or Jacqueline Bouvier Kennedy were to femininity in their time—icons of class, grace, charm, style, beauty, and nobility.

4

Even Reveille's physical features conjure regal images and reflections. Her flowing, golden-brown hair and white-tuft neckline resemble a Victorian-age robe fit for a queen. And on the sprawling Texas A&M campus, Reveille is certainly more of a princess than a pooch. Her custom-made blanket, which drapes across her back and snaps under her belly, is adorned with five diamonds, symbolic of her status as the highest-ranking member of the university's Corps of Cadets. She has access to any building on campus, attends virtually every football game and many other sporting events, travels in style, lives and sleeps in the corps dorms, attends classes, and occasionally determines when those classes should end. From the days of the original Rev, she has been called the "Queen" or the "First Lady of Texas A&M," a campus where tradition is rooted as deeply as the oak trees that have stood since the university was first opened in 1876 as a land-grant college near the banks of the Brazos River.

From Silver Taps to the 12th Man and from Muster to March-in, Texas A&M resonates with a passionate appreciation for all of its traditions, but Reveille strikes a chord with the students and former students of A&M like no other tradition. In fact, Reveille even reaches people who have little to no appreciation or preference for Texas A&M or its traditions. Reveille may be treated like royalty in College Station, but the appeal of this American collie transcends school pride. She connects with virtually anyone whose imagination was captured by Lad, the collie made famous by Albert Payson Terhune's books in the 1920s and '30s. And for the millions of Americans who grew up with Lassie—the books, the movies, and the television show—the sight of

Reveille VI battled epileptic seizures throughout much of her life, a condition veterinarians combated with Phenobarbital. The drug reduced the occurrences of the seizures and prolonged her ability to serve as the mascot, but the constant medications also took their toll on her liver. Courtesy Texas A&M Sports Information

5

Let's Get Outta Here

One of the things that makes Reveille particularly unusual among all other university mascots is that she attends class with the student body of Texas A&M. Most often, Rev greets a few students around her and goes to sleep until the lecture is complete. But like many of the students she represents, Rev occasionally becomes bored with lengthy lectures and speaks out.

According to A&M tradition, when Reveille barks in class, the professor is supposed to pack up the lesson plan and give the class a walk. Even today, many of the professors—especially those with A&M ties or an appreciation of Aggie traditions—still honor the walk-for-bark tradition.

"Oh yeah," said Kevin Graham, the Mascot Corporal in 1999–2000. "I even got out of a test one time. The professor was passing the test out, and she had passed it out to about five people in a class of one hundred or so when Rev barked. We got a walk. The professor said that we were going to put it off until Monday. She gave people the option of taking it right then if they were ready to take it, but there were at least half the people in that class who were instant Reveille fans. Probably a lot of them had a little too much fun on Thursday night and weren't ready to take the test. But she didn't usually bark much. One week—I don't know what was going on—I got out of class three times. She got a lot of treats that week. There were always people trying to get her to bark. It was pretty funny."

While some professors do not necessarily appreciate Reveille in their classroom, others go to great lengths to welcome her. "I went in for a geology final at the very end of my freshman year, when I had Rev for about a month," Graham said. "The prof comes in and passes out the test and says good luck and leaves. We're all wondering where he went, and he comes back ten minutes later with another test and an ink pad. He comes and kneels down next to my desk and opens the ink pad up and puts Rev's foot on the ink. Then he puts her paw print on the test. When we came back to the building a couple days later to check our grades before we left for the summer, it had everybody's social security number and their grades. But right at the top it said 'Reveille' and had 100 by her score. It had the photocopy of the exam with her paw print on it. I don't know if she ruined the curve for everybody or not."

And in perhaps the best example of a professor welcoming Reveille to the classroom, accounting professor Annie McGowan received allergy shots all summer once she discovered Mascot Corporal Graham was enrolled in her class. "Apparently, [McGowan] was extremely allergic to dogs," Graham said. "So, she spent the whole summer taking allergy shots just so she could have Rev in her class. She called roll that first day, and after I said, 'here,' she told me she had been taking the allergy shots so that Rev could be in the class. That's a pretty serious commitment."

Reveille V's breeder in Del Rio initially named her "Maybe," because he knew she would be considered as the possible mascot of Texas A&M. Courtesy Texas A&M Sports Information

Reveille is akin to a brush with greatness. "It's not just Aggies who are lining up to have their picture taken with Reveille," said Jordan Caddick, who as a sophomore in 2002–2003 served as Company E-2's Mascot Corporal and Reveille's constant companion. "I can't tell you how many times during the course of a year when we were traveling in airports, hotels, and so forth that I would hear little kids say, 'Look, Mommy, there's Lassie.' There's no doubt in my mind that the lasting popularity of Lassie has increased Reveille's national appeal. And the image of Lassie, always by her owner's side or looking out for her owner's best interest, has helped a lot, too."

Reveille turns heads and attracts a crowd wherever she goes on campus. Mascot handlers often leave for class an hour early just to allow for all the stops she makes for students who pat and pose with her. Here, Reveille VII is greeted by two students at the MSC Bookstore. Courtesy Trey Wright

Indeed, it has. But Reveille is not about a particular breed, either. She is representative of a timeless bond between man and his best friend. She is the living, breathing, tail-wagging embodiment of loyalty, companionship, servitude, playfulness, and unconditional love. Those qualities, of course, do not make her particularly unique among the burgeoning canine population in this country. According to Norma Bennett Woolf, editor of the *Dog Owner's Guide,* an online magazine, there are approximately sixty million dogs that receive veterinary care in the United States in roughly thirty-seven million households. Most of those canine owners would probably describe their own pets by using the exact same list of qualities. What makes Reveille one in sixty million, however, is her lifestyle, accessibility, and the indelible mark the tradition of this mascot has left on thousands of A&M students since the early 1930s.

You do not necessarily need to wear an Aggie ring or swell with maroon pride to fall in love with Reveille and the tradition that encompasses her. All you really need is an affection for fur, slobbery kisses, and paw prints on the back porch. If you cried with Old Yeller, laughed with Benji, or embraced Rin Tin Tin, the story of Reveille—and the evolution of the tradition—will undoubtedly touch your heart. If you have ever mourned the death of a family dog, spent countless hours in the back yard tossing a drool-covered tennis ball or stick, stopped your car to attend to a stray, or knelt in welcoming anticipation of a long, friendly lick on the cheek, this is a story and a tradition that you will almost certainly admire. At its essence, this tradition is not about just supporting a team but also the

Reveille VII, adorned in her patriotic mum, stands at midfield before the A&M–Oklahoma State game in 2001. Rev joined more than 75,000 fans in paying tribute to those who died in the September 11 terrorist attacks. Photo by Mark Beal, courtesy Texas A&M University Relations

According to legend, Reveille received her name after responding enthusiastically to the bugler's morning rendition of reveille. Courtesy Cushing Library

stories of how they came to be the mascots of their particular schools are not extraordinary. At Tennessee, for example, the students in 1953 simply decided they wanted a live mascot. They conducted a poll, and at halftime of a football game later that year, Smokey, a blue tick hound dog, was selected from among other dogs as the Tennessee mascot by the ovation level of the crowd.

The original Reveille, on the other hand, earned her way into the hearts of Aggieland. Besides, Reveille has always played an integral role in the day-to-day life of the student body she represents. Reveille is not simply the athletic teams' mascot (it's not the Texas A&M Collies, after all). Nor does she belong exclusively to Company E-2, the Corps of Cadets unit that cares for her every need. She belongs, in principle, to the entire student body of Texas A&M, which now numbers nearly forty-five thousand students. As such, she is a visible part of university life throughout the year. She doesn't simply show up at a stadium on game days or appear only at school fund-raising functions, as Uga, Smokey (both of whom live in private homes), and many of the other mascots do. Reveille doesn't live on campus in a cage; she resides inside the dorm, occasionally on a cadet's bed. You don't need a sideline press pass to touch her; she attends classes with the students every day of the week, jogs with Company E-2, and is even welcomed into the Corps of Cadets mess hall and restaurants throughout the community. Reveille also owns a personalized student identification card, her own cell phone (the Mascot Corporal does the actual dialing and speaking), and her own credit card to cover travel expenses.

belief that a dog can enrich the lives of people, breaking up the monotony of everyday life with a consistent warmth and wagging tail.

Other schools have canine mascots, of course. In fact, *Sports Illustrated* in 1997 placed Uga, the bulldog mascot of the University of Georgia, on the cover of the magazine and selected Uga as the number one mascot in the United States. Washington, Mississippi State, Fresno State, Louisiana Tech, Tennessee, and various other universities also possess canine mascots that appear on the sidelines of football games or the courtside of basketball games. But by and large, the

"Reveille is a lot of different things to a lot of different people," said Jeff Heath, Mascot Corporal to Reveille V in 1992–93. "But maybe one of the most important roles she serves is as the dog the students left behind when they came to campus. She becomes everyone's dog at Texas A&M, and even if the students just occasionally see her on the way to class or have a chance to pose with her for a picture, there's a bond formed with her. To me, Texas A&M is a special place for many, many reasons. But I absolutely believe it would not be the same place without Reveille. She brings something very special and unique to the campus that is irreplaceable."

That is obviously why A&M officials are willing to go to such great lengths—financially and as the crow flies—to find the healthiest prospective puppy on the planet. The search for Reveille VII, for example, took A&M from Central Texas to Fort Lauderdale, where Dr. Cindi Bossart, a veterinarian, and her husband, James Efron, were receiving national acclaim for canine reproduction and genetic testing and counseling. Ultimately, Reveille VII's mother was artificially inseminated by mixing the semen of two championship male collies. With the aid of genetic technology, it was later determined which male actually served as Reveille's father. Her mother is a Westminster Kennel Club champion and comes from a line of multiple best-in-show winners. One of her uncles was the top collie in the country for the three years prior to Reveille's birth, and another uncle was the top collie the year before that. So, for four consecutive years, the top collie in the United States was directly related to Reveille VII.

"Her blood lines are impeccable," said Bossart, who has also served as chairman of the Collie Club of America's Health Committee. "What makes her even more unique is the fact that she was the only puppy of what we assumed would be a full litter. Her mother had litters of nine or ten puppies, but with Reveille, there was only one. That's very rare. In my mind, that says something about her destiny to be Reveille, the chosen one."

Reveille VII may have been the purest of pure breeds, the best of the best, and the most genetically perfect collie in the country. But in her role as Reveille, she is also related—at least by association and kindred spirit—to the original mutt who started it all back in the 1930s. The first Reveille's blood lines were about as pure as the air around a petroleum plant. She was a vagabond and undoubtedly the product of an era when spaying or neutering was deemed unnecessary or too expensive. The original Reveille may have been a relatively cute puppy—what puppy isn't?—but as she aged, her once-shiny, black coat dulled to a dingy mix of black, brown, and white, while her face became a beard of black and gray hair and her torso rounded. To put it mildly, the original Rev was not going to win any beauty contests. "She was a mongrel mutt in every sense," said Howard Shelton, who played on the Aggies' 1939 national championship football team and frequently observed the original Reveille roaming the campus. "She was definitely not an attractive dog. But that didn't matter to any of us. A&M wasn't that attractive back then, either. What mattered was that that little dog seemed to believe that she had some kind of special purpose on the campus. She belonged to us, and she seemed to realize that we all belonged to her."

A Day in the Life of Reveille

A typical non-game day for Reveille and her Mascot Corporal (from Jerred Crumley, the Mascot Corporal in 2003–2004)

0530: Wake up and prepare for morning activity
0600: Morning activity (usually a run)
0650: Formation with the entire corps
0710: Breakfast in Duncan Dining Hall
0725: Fix and serve Reveille her breakfast in the room
0730–0830: Prepare for class
0830: Leave the dorm for class
0900: Class
1030: Go back to the dorm
1100: Play in the room or sleep
1200–0330: Usually open for Reveille events, other classes, or Reveille appearances
0400: Afternoon activity or class (usually drill or athletics)
0600: Evening formation with the entire corps
0615: Dinner in Duncan
0645: Fix and serve Reveille her dinner in the room
0700–1000: Study time
1030: Go to bed

UNCERTAIN ORIGINS

No Aggie—then or now—denies, contradicts, or questions that Reveille I possessed the disposition of an angel, the personality of a saint, and the nurturing nature of a blue-haired grandma. But her initial arrival on the A&M campus is quite a source of debate. In fact, dying men literally went to their graves willing to take a lie detector test to prove that they either knew or participated in the real origins of Reveille. Files in the Texas A&M University Archives contain dozens of versions crediting at least ten different sources with bringing Reveille to campus. Through University Archives and other published reports, at least thirty-six people publicly claimed to have been involved in bringing the first Reveille to campus.

The most popular and widely accepted version of the story recounts how several Aggies returning from a Navasota bar (the town is some twenty miles south of College Station) late one night in 1931 accidentally hit a small puppy with their Model T. The cadets backtracked and found the dog wounded but wagging her tail. According to legend, they put the dog in the car and smuggled her back into their dorm, Leggett Hall, which violated university policies regarding pets in the rooms. As the story goes, the cadets bandaged the pup that night, and when the dog awoke the next morning to the sound of the bugler blasting Reveille, she barked enthusiastically. Her reaction to the bugle call inspired the cadets to name her "Reveille."

That's the neat, tidy tale that has been told, printed in official university publications, and immortalized throughout the years. It may even be true. But other

In the mid-1930s, cadets found a dog that they believed could serve as Reveille's successor. The cadets named the dog Retreat, but Rev did not take kindly to him and chased him off campus. Here, Rev shows a little more compassion toward a stray cat.
Courtesy Cushing Library

versions raise alternative possibilities. Jerry Cooper's article in the *Texas Aggie,* the official publication of A&M's Association of Former Students, recounts several other renditions:

- J. W. Batts, class of '35, claimed that Reveille was smuggled onto campus by him and Madero Bader, '32, after they found her at a truck stop in Hempstead while hitchhiking back from Galveston.
- Class of 1934 members Johnny Mitchell, Jim Wallace, John E. Weaver, and C. D. Long submitted a story in which a small black dog was picked up on a punishment march to the Brazos River by the A and B field artillery batteries.

The original Reveille's blanket, worn in the 1930s by the black and white mutt who started the tradition, has been on display in the Texas A&M Lettermen's Association Athletic Museum. Courtesy Trey Wright

- Asa B. Gibbs, '37, claimed that he and Ross Reid, '34, found Reveille in a ditch near Northgate (on the perimeter of the main campus), the apparent victim of an automobile accident.
- Bob Norwood, '35, said that he and his roommate found Reveille in a ditch between the old Boyett's service station and Walton Hall. In Norwood's version, she wasn't injured, only wet and hungry.
- Eddie Chew, who served as an assistant groundskeeper for the A&M athletic department, claimed that Reveille was born at his home south of campus. In 1940, Chew said he didn't tell his story at the time because, "she had such a good home . . . and seemed so happy, and the boys all liked her. It sure made me happy to think the boys would want any dog I ever owned. And just look at how famous she is now. If I would have kept her, she never would have got anywhere."
- Perhaps the most compelling and detailed version of Rev's arrival belonged to George Comnas, '35, who delivered his Muster speech in 1980 on "the origins of the first Reveille." Comnas said he found Reveille in January of 1932 after he hitchhiked back from Houston. "In returning to campus late on Saturday night, I disembarked from a cotton truck at the old railroad station between the drill grounds and the horse stables," Comnas said in his speech. "Along

the side of the road, I saw a little whimpering animal, which was a small, nondescript dog principally of fox terrier bloodlines with some other mongrel blood. She had been hit by a car and was lying in a ditch whimpering more out of fright than out of injury."

According to Comnas, he and about twenty-five to thirty other cadets who were arriving at the old highway gate across from the railroad station encircled the dog. The cadets were arriving by trucks, Model Ts, and so forth. Comnas claimed that he took the wounded puppy back to Leggett Hall and was assisted by Bob Anderson, who was both his next-door neighbor and a veterinary student, in bandaging her injured leg and setting her hip in place. Living in a cardboard box underneath Comnas's bed at night and hiding in the baggage room on the lower floor of the dormitory during the day, the dog quickly recovered. Within four or five days after finding her, Comnas began taking her out onto the streets to join the Corps of Cadets for morning exercises. By the midterm break of that semester, the dog was a constant companion during those morning exercises. "I unconsciously said to the B-Troop Cavalry one day, 'Here comes our Reveille,' referring to the bugle call for Reveille that occurred just about the same time we were doing our exercises," Comnas recalled. "The name stuck, and our pet became the pet of the Cavalry and then the pet of the band. . . . I did not realize at the time that Reveille had become a symbol of the attitude of love and affection that an animal can have for man, and man for an animal."

Comnas, who went on to gain an international reputation in the shipping and marketing of petroleum products and other commodities and was later named as a Texas A&M Distinguished Alumnus, cited the names of four fellow students in his speech who could corroborate his story. Comnas even provided their home cities if anyone in the audience wanted to follow up. Following his speech in 1980, Comnas wrote many letters to university officials and spent a considerable amount of time attempting to convince anyone who would listen that his version was the authentic one.

Perhaps the varying accounts of the origins of Reveille can be attributed to two things: 1) She was so beloved that many people desired to lay claim to her—and possibly convinced themselves of playing a role in her discovery; and 2) she was such a vagabond that there was at least some truth to many of the versions. In a 1990 letter to Jerry Cooper, Dr. Mavis P. Kelsey, who would also receive acclaim as a Texas A&M Distinguished Alumnus, provided some insight to the possibilities of the varying accounts of Reveille's origin. Dr. Kelsey wrote to Cooper:

I read with a great deal of interest your fine article . . . about the origin of the first Reveille. I've always been interested in Reveille's origins and wanted to report what I knew about them.

After reading your article, I believe several people "discovered" this same dog on different occasions before she became famous. I see no reason to doubt that Reveille was born on Eddie Chew's place, as Eddie claims.

15

Always ready to play, Reveille I roamed the campus freely in search of lonely, homesick cadets. When she found them, she practically made them play fetch with her. Courtesy Cushing Library

I saw this exact dog several times running around the campus between the YMCA and Sbisa Hall where I was a "volunteer." I considered her to be a young, stray dog and used to pet her because she was very friendly and occasionally followed me to the dormitory where I lived across the hall from my friend Madero Bader (who seems to be one of Reveille's several discoverers).

For quite a while practically no one paid any attention to this dog who tried to be friendly. Then the dog started following the band and greeting people at the mess hall, and the next thing I knew, this exact same dog was known to everyone; and everyone vied for her attention; and she was called Reveille. I felt proud to have known Reveille when she was just a little, stray dog before she became the famous mascot.

That letter may go a long way toward explaining why so many different people believed they had a claim to Reveille. But in the broad scope of the tradition, it probably doesn't really matter who actually brought the first Reveille to campus. What matters most is that the little black dog with white feet and a golden heart brought warmth to a campus that was in grave need of any source of compassion.

Texas A&M in the early 1930s was, in a word, stark. The drab campus was located ninety miles northwest of Houston and must have seemed like a million miles from true affection. Sure, there was an incredible camaraderie among the roughly five thousand students, but without a woman's touch, warmth came only in the form of a wool blanket, while compassion was only an occasional weekend visitor. The all-male, all-military Agricultural and Mechanical College of Texas may have been located in the sunbelt, but its environment was cold and rigid. And to make matters worse, the stock market crash of 1929 made things even bleaker.

Enter Reveille, who was forty-something pounds of pure compassion, warmth, and unconditional love. She also was female, a fact that should not be overlooked on a totally masculine campus. Considering the times and the conditions of the campus, it's really not so difficult to envision how she so quickly endeared herself to the cadets. Almost from the start, the dog seemed like a perfect fit at A&M. For one thing, A&M had a distinguished veterinary school on campus, and man's best friend at an all-male school just felt right. In all likelihood, an ordinary, run-of-the-mill dog would not have made such a lasting impression. While Reveille didn't have a pedigree, she was definitely not ordinary.

After being initially smuggled into the dorms and being fed with table scraps from the mess hall, Reveille, for all intents and purposes, was turned loose. Instead of wandering away, she watched and learned. She roamed the four thousand acres of the A&M campus on her own and quickly learned that anyone in a khaki uniform was her friend, while those in civilian clothes should be viewed in a less trusting light. She also learned when and where to appear for "mess formation," as she marched with the cadets into mess hall for meals. According to an article by H. B. McElroy in

In addition to her loving, playful spirit, Reveille seemed to embody characteristics that the all-male, all-military college held so dearly, including loyalty, camaraderie, and service. Courtesy Cushing Library

the *Battalion,* the school newspaper, one of Reveille's first forays into the mess hall was met with resistance by one of the waiters. As the waiter prepared to catch the dog and throw her out, four cadets cornered the waiter and threatened to run him out instead. From that point on, Reveille had free rein of the mess hall and every other building on campus, as well.

Whenever she tired, Reveille would wander into any dormitory, hunt for an open door, and hop onto the lower bunk bed. It was during the early 1930s when the tradition regarding Reveille on the bed first began. Originally, it was noted that if a cadet found Reveille on his bed, he was not to dislodge her. If she chose to spend the night in that bed, the cadet was to find another bed, sleep on the floor, or pull the desks together and bunk on the hardwood. To some degree, that tradition still holds true today, but it's been modified over the years.

"We had bunk beds you could knock up higher and higher," said Kevin Graham, Mascot Corporal for Reveille VI in 1999–2000. "The lowest of the beds was probably four feet high in our room, so Rev couldn't get up in it by herself. So, I never officially got kicked out of my bed. But a couple of times I did put her up on the bed, and I slept on the floor just so when people asked me I could honestly say that, 'Yes, I slept on the floor because Rev was in my bed.' And once she was there, she wasn't moving. Nobody really has to sleep on the floor anymore, but it's a part of the legacy started by the first Reveille."

In the public eye, perhaps the first Reveille's number-one legacy was established at a football game during the fall of 1932 when she made the first formation with the Aggie band on Kyle field, prancing in front of the drum major to the roar of the crowd. Reveille seemed to feed off the energy of the band and frolicked to the approval of the crowd. It was an impromptu move by the dog, but it was also the moment that officially earned her the designation as the school's mascot.

In more private settings, however, Reveille made her most lasting impact through the individual contacts she made with cadets. By the mid-1930s, Reveille was well-known on campus for the uncanny, canine sixth sense she displayed time and time again. She would seek out unhappy, lonely Aggies—many of them freshman cadets away from home for the first time ever—and continually attempt to cheer them up by bringing them a stick and practically demanding that they participate in a friendly game of fetch. According to several published reports, Reveille would rarely accept "no" for an answer when it came to accompanying anyone in khaki. "We kept her in the Veterinary Hospital in the spring of 1932," said W. Z. Burke, DVM, in an article written by Haynes W. Dugan, class of 1934. "We kept her [in the hospital] for a couple months after surgery [to be spayed]. During that time, it was easy to notice that she was a dog that apparently loved everyone. In all my years of practice, I have seen a few dogs with her love for people, but none that showed it more."

The first Reveille, indeed, was something of a saint, bouncing from dorm to dorm, building to building, and room to room in search of the lonely, lost, and love-starved. And as she made her rounds throughout campus, the cadets became more and more protective of her. According to a 1940 article in the *Battalion,* Rev

Another tradition is born, as Reveille I takes the bed of a senior cadet. According to legend, if Rev hopped into a cadet's bed, the young man was supposed to find another place to sleep. That tradition has been modified through the years, as cadets are now allowed to share their bed with Miss Reveille. Courtesy Cushing Library

had begun making out-of-town corps trips by the mid-1930s, requiring a seat by herself on the train. On a particular trip when the train was so crowded that passengers were forced to stand in the aisles, the conductor discovered Reveille with a seat to herself. "Get that damn dog off the seat and let a passenger sit down," the conductor said as he made his way through the passenger area. Within seconds, approximately ten A&M cadets threatened to throw him off his own train. The conductor retreated, and Reveille rode the rest of the way in comfort, while many others stood. Later in her life, according to another article in the

According to university archives and other published reports, at least thirty-six people claimed to play a role in bringing the original Reveille to campus. Courtesy Cushing Library

Battalion, a conductor actually removed Reveille from a train and left her at the station. But cadets on board caused such a stir—and made so many threats—that the conductor agreed, in fear for his own safety, to put the train in reverse for several miles to pick her up. When the train returned to the station, Reveille was waiting patiently, as if she knew it would be only a matter of moments before her cadets came to the rescue. When the train backed into the station, she jumped on board and into an empty seat that had been vacated for her.

By 1934, the cadets were so enamored of Reveille that they began making plans for a possible replacement. Since no one could confirm her age—and since her face was already beginning to gray—several Aggies searched for and found a puppy that looked similar to the original Reveille and positioned him as the next possible mascot. The cadets named the young, male puppy "Retreat" (for the bugle call played at sunset). Unfortunately, they did not consult with Reveille before bringing Retreat on duty. Within a few weeks of Retreat's arrival, Reveille effectively ran the new puppy off campus for good, forcing his resignation before Retreat's reign could ever begin. Reveille was a loving dog, but she wasn't willing to share her spotlight with another canine.

Besides, Reveille's aggressiveness toward Retreat was another indication that she wasn't ready to slow down. She had plenty of life left in her, and she became even more of a fixture on campus throughout the decade. She received free veterinary care on campus, annually received a new maroon and white blanket for her public appearances (although she despised wearing it and eventually figured out how to slip out of it), and delighted in running through the band as it performed on the field. Reveille even made several cameo appearances

Following her cameo appearance in the movie We've Never Been Licked, *a female viewer wrote the Aggie Corps to suggest that Reveille be made a general in the K-9 unit of the WAGS division of Dogs for Defense. It was the first official ranking for Reveille, who is today the highest-ranking member of the corps.* Courtesy Cushing Library

Following her death on January 18, 1943, Reveille I received full military honors at her funeral. She was buried just outside the old horseshoe at the north end of Kyle Field.
Courtesy Cushing Library

in the 1943 Hollywood movie, *We've Never Been Licked,* which was filmed partly on the A&M campus.

When she did finally begin to slow down in the early 1940s, the Corps of Cadets decided to immortalize Reveille through the WAGS division of Dogs for Defense. With World War II raging overseas, any dog owner in the United States could purchase a rank for his dog. The donation ranged from one dollar for a private to one hundred dollars for a general's commission. Because of her importance on a military campus, a drive was launched among the students in the summer of 1943 to obtain the necessary funds to make Reveille a general. Even in difficult economic times, and with A&M's enrollment greatly reduced because of the number of

Aggies serving in World War II, the cadets opened their wallets to honor Reveille. Not only was enough money raised for her new ranking, but the student body also commissioned Marie Haynes, a talented local artist of national acclaim, to paint a portrait of Reveille. The painting was unveiled during the Aggie Bonfire in 1943, the night before the annual Thanksgiving Day football showdown against the University of Texas.

In an unveiling speech, university president Dr. Frank C. Bolton pointed out that Reveille's importance on campus was not only symbolic of Texas A&M's value system but was also a defining difference of America's wartime values. Referencing Germany, Bolton said that a "nation that can callously destroy men, women, and children for the sole reason that they are a different racial stock" would not understand this reverence for Reveille. "But we have shown them," Bolton continued, "that with all our reverence for womanhood, our respect for the individual, and even our kindness for dumb animals, we can and will fight all the more earnestly for our ideals and the right to continue them. We have shown them that as a nation we do not have to be hard-hearted to maintain our existence. Reveille is more than an animal. She is a tradition . . . a tangible, visible connecting link with carefree boyhood. I am happy to unveil this painting, a tribute to ten thousand masters. May it preserve to future generations of Aggies the tradition of Reveille, a faithful, lovable dog."

Not even a full two months later—on January 18, 1944—Reveille's tail finally stopped wagging. The lovable mutt, who seemed to sense that she had a higher purpose to serve than most other dogs, took her last breath in the A&M Veterinary Hospital. On the follow-

The bronzed statue of the original Reveille is located in the Sam Houston Sanders Corps of Cadets Center. The statue was paid for by members of the classes of 1933–36 and was delivered to the Corps Center shortly after it opened in 1992. Courtesy Vannessa Burson

ing day, the entire Corps of Cadets, several hundred former students who were back at A&M for military training, and numerous residents in the Bryan–College Station area poured into Kyle field for a full military funeral for Aggieland's little lady. She was laid to rest (in an infant's casket lined with maroon velvet) just outside the north end zone of the stadium. Her death and funeral made international news, reaching servicemen around the world and generating a flood of consoling telegrams, letters, and flowers. Among the most touching of the tributes was a poem by Dr. John Ashton, which appeared in the *Battalion* two days after her death. Ashton's verse seemed to sum up the feelings of a mourning campus:

GOOD-BYE REVEILLE

When "dress parade" once more comes
  around;
And grass grows green o'er tiny mound;
We'll think of one we'll ne'er more see;
Our darling little Reveille!

Ancestral claims she boasted not;
Poor mongrel waif—such was her lot.
But campus days were all serene
When homeless pup became a "queen."

In doggie languagem, plain as day,
Rev warned all canines: "Keep away,
This is my show, I'll search no more;
No other dog shall lead this corps."

So when the band struck up an air
We always knew that Rev was there,
For sure enough, her bark of glee
As good as meant, "Just look at me."

. . .

She pranced and capered, yelped with joy;
No lady dog e'er looked so coy.
Her funny antics, born of zeal,
Won hosts of friends thru sheer appeal.

To Rev all Aggies smelled the same,
Whate'er their rank or whence they came.
She loved them all with equal zest;
They honored her as welcome guest.

But now she's sailed on Charon's barge;
No more we hear her bark at large.
Her work is done, now let her rest:
If dogs have souls, may hers be blest!

In the days and months that followed her death, there was talk on campus of finding a new mascot. But to many of the cadets, planning for a replacement seemed almost disrespectful to Reveille's memory. It also went against the nature of how the first Reveille came to be. "The birth of the [Reveille] tradition was never planned nor conceived," Comnas wrote in a 1988 letter. "It just grew up out of a lot of coincidences such as the puppy attaching itself to the cadets and they, in turn, returned that love and adopted her through a gradual evolution of events—Corps trips, a campus home, football games, and the ubiquitous military band."

There was a sentiment throughout 1944 and for much of the rest of the decade that no other dog would ever do. No other canine could ever fill the paw prints left by the little mutt with the big heart, the dog that filled a drab campus with life and made it feel so much more like a home.

CHAPTER 2

Good Company

E-2 AT THE OTHER END OF THE LEASH

IRREVERENTLY and intrusively, the deep-rooted, jagged-edged weeds and crabgrass enjoyed some twenty years of unchecked growth, covering the tiny grave and engulfing even the ring of white rocks that marked the original Reveille's burial site. Even after the presentation of Reveille II in 1952, which renewed A&M's mascot traditions, the grave of the first Reveille was neglected. By 1965, her resting spot had become so obscure and unattractive that considerable confusion existed among many Texas A&M students regarding the precise location of her remains. Some believed she was actually buried inside Kyle Field; others assumed she'd been placed beneath the large, pink granite block "T" that bore her name and stood along the outer wall of the horseshoe in the north end zone. In reality, though, the neglected burial site was located across the pavement that once surrounded the horseshoe.

Her legacy was still strong on campus, but the grave hardly befitted the honor in which she was still held. "There wasn't a marker for her grave, and the area surrounding it was just plain ugly," said Andrew Salge, the Mascot Corporal for Reveille II in 1963–64 and the company commander of E-2 in '66. "It was in sad shape. Nothing really had been done to it since Reveille I died in 1944. As the unit that cared for Reveille, we just felt like something really needed to be done."

Something was done. Something special, as a matter of fact. Ever since the mid-1950s, when Reveille has been in need of anything, Company E-2 (Rebel-E)—and formerly known as A Company Quartermaster—has quickly answered the call. In this particular 1966 case, the outfit cleaned up the site, plucked the weeds, and formed a committee of "fish" (freshmen) to visit

Reveille III, the first American collie in the line of A&M mascots, appears to be eager to assume the duties from her predecessor, Reveille II, in this mid-1960s pose. Courtesy Cushing Library

local memorial companies to inquire about the prices of tombstones. Upon hearing the purpose of the stone, one sympathetic owner cut the price from sixty-five dollars to fifty dollars. "The committee collected the money—$2 from each of the 25 fish—in just two days," 1966 E-2 freshman Bill Jones told the *Battalion*. "Everybody in the freshman class [of E-2] had an equal hand in it."

With the granite headstone purchased, the freshmen "appropriated" some leftover bricks in a daring midnight raid from a pile behind President James Earl Rudder's home on campus. They removed the weatherbeaten rocks and replaced them with a brick-paved memorial that surrounded the new marker. "We felt like a bunch of brand new fathers," Jones told the *Battalion*. "This was something that was purely our own—none of the upperclassmen even knew about it for several days. From now on, it's going to be a traditional fish privilege of this outfit to take care of the gravesite."

It was, indeed, a significant improvement that put the gravesite in a new perspective for all of Aggieland. Where weeds once ruled, Reveille I was now memorialized to all the students, fans, and onlookers who entered Kyle Field through the north gate. The tribute by the freshmen even earned the praises of the upperclassmen in E-2. "It was the best thing the Rebel E fish have done to improve morale, and it's certainly something they can be proud of forever," Salge said at the time.

It didn't even matter that the appropriated bricks could have been considered "stolen" or that the headstone was replaced several months later because the "Reveille" engraving had been misspelled. What mattered was that E-2 once again came to Reveille's rescue, honoring her memory and enhancing the tradition. In Rev's life and in her death, E-2 has consistently gone to extraordinary means to preserve, protect, and celebrate the canine's place in Texas A&M's past, present, and future. While the entire Cadet Corps embraces the motto, "Keepers of the Spirit," E-2 also serves as the caretakers of the living, breathing, barking symbol of the Aggie spirit. It is an honor that most members of the outfit find difficult to describe, but one that they cherish for the rest of their lives. Many of the Mascot Corporals begin with the intent of serving the university, but somewhere along the way they inevitably fall in love with the tradition and the dog.

"I went to A&M not knowing a lot about the university, and I was lucky enough to get in the same outfit that had Reveille, then got lucky enough to be chosen as the Mascot Corporal," said Jeff Gruetzmacker, Reveille IV's handler in 1977–78. "If I could go back today and do it all over again, I wouldn't change a thing. It was such a blessing in so many ways. In fact, the woman I'm married to now went on our first date because of Reveille. . . . As we started dating, I did assure her that, at the end of the year, the dog would be gone and it would just be me that she had to deal with. But I guess I was solid enough to be my wife's consolation prize."

Being seen with Reveille obviously does have its advantages. But there are numerous sacrifices and inconveniences, too. While Reveille may be a "chick magnet," she is also a tremendous time consumer. Kevin Graham, the Mascot Corporal in 1999–2000, estimates that he put sixteen thousand miles on his vehicle in one summer as he and Reveille VI attended approximately forty-five Aggie Moms' Clubs meetings, the summer football coaches tour, howdy parties, new student conferences, fish camp, and other A&M functions. Rick Holcomb, Reveille V's handler in 1986–87, is one of many Mascot Corporals who can recall the night—or, in some cases, the many nights—he spent cleaning up diarrhea, vomit, and so forth. Bob Vanderberry, the Mascot Corporal in 1975–76, first endured the agony of Reveille III's death, watching helplessly as the aging dog's organs painstakingly shut down. Vanderberry then experienced the thrill of caring for Rev IV as a puppy, but part of that "fun" was finding tiny teeth marks on practically everything he owned. Polishing out scuffs is one thing; massaging out molar indentations is quite another. Unlike other puppies, you wouldn't dare simply toss Reveille outside or confine her to a cage for punishment. And pity the poor fool who even thinks about swatting Rev with a rolled newspaper. All training with Reveille is expected to be done with positive reinforcement.

The simple logistics of a good-sized dog sharing a small dorm room with two teenaged boys creates its own set of nuisances, as well. It's difficult to maintain the spit-and-polish image of the Corps of Cadets with dog hair constantly covering everything you own. Collies shed like a Christmas tree dropping its needles in late February. Rev's daily grooming alone is a tedious, time-consuming job, and serving as her handler is a twenty-four-hour, seven-days-a-week responsibility that requires expert time management skills. After all, she is never to be left alone, and she is always on the Mascot Corporal's mind. In essence, the Mascot Corporal lives for one full year in a state of constant concern, with nagging concern for Rev's health, safety, and well-being.

Fortunately for the handler, the care of the collie is not a one-man operation. Help is provided in the form of an entire class of Reveille fanatics. Ultimately, the whole sophomore class of E-2 is responsible for her care and is at her constant beck and call. With her current popularity, it probably wouldn't work any other way.

"It is far too big a job for one person," Graham said. "As much as I could, Rev was with me. We were pretty much joined at the hip twenty-four hours a day. But there were times when one thing or another happened and I either couldn't take her where she needed to be or I needed to be somewhere where I couldn't take her. Fortunately, I had thirty-two other guys in my class who I knew I could count on. Every Sunday night, I would meet with our sophomore class, and I would stand up and tell everybody Rev's schedule for the week. For example: Monday afternoon she needs to be at an elementary school for a test rally, and Monday night she has to be at a basketball game; Tuesday morning she is taking bridal pictures; Wednesday she is going to be at a volleyball game; Thursday we are in Houston for a Mothers' Club meeting; and Friday we're leaving town for the football game. That's a typical week. So, I would stand up and say, 'I need three guys to be at all these things.' Or if I had a test on Wednesday night, I would tell them I needed three people to be at the volleyball game for me. That's when it was huge to have that kind of support."

While the sophomores are the prime providers, the freshmen are the menial task force. One of the primary responsibilities of E-2 freshmen is to provide a protective wall around Reveille following football games, especially away football games where the environment can be hostile toward the Aggies. The human wall encircles Reveille and the Mascot Corporal immediately after the contest and escorts them to the corps dorms following home games or to their means of transportation following away games. It's not uncommon for the freshmen to be pelted with batteries, water bottles, beer cans, or other projectiles while shielding Reveille from harm's way on the road. Most often, Reveille emerges unscathed or, at worst, with some cola stains on her normally pristine coat. But there have been particularly harrowing experiences when opposing fans stormed the field in pursuit of the goal posts and sought Reveille as a prize. In those cases, the Aggie band usually forms a secondary ring around the freshmen to provide further assistance. In most stadiums and on most game days, such protective measures aren't necessary. But on road trips within the state of Texas—where the passion of a rivalry can turn downright bloodthirsty—the E-2 freshmen are especially on guard.

"Deep in my heart, I truly believe that the vast majority of people—no matter who they are rooting for—would never want to hurt a dog that is so full of love," said Jeff Bailey, the Mascot Corporal for Reveille VI in 1997–98. "But people sometimes get caught up in the heat of the moment and lose sight of the fact that she is a dog and focus only on the fact that she is a symbol of Texas A&M. It can get scary. All you're thinking

Although the well-known tradition allows for Reveille to sleep on any bed she chooses, several of the collies preferred the den-like confines of the closet. Here, Rev VI snuggles on top of Kevin Graham's shoes, which allowed Graham to sleep in his own bed. Courtesy Kevin Graham

Through the years, Reveille has been almost as constant a figure on the A&M campus as the towering oak trees. Photo by Mark Beal, courtesy Texas A&M University Relations

30

about is protecting Reveille. At a time like that you are just so thankful for your freshmen and the band and whoever else is there willing to lend you an escape method. We give the freshmen a lot of grief during their first year, but they are really on their toes when duty calls."

Of course, freshmen in E-2 must also be on their toes on a day-to-day basis. Fish are allowed to know, as well as speak, the word "canine," but they are not permitted to know, let alone speak, the word "dog." Fish are not allowed to let their eyes linger on Reveille, and they must greet her with a respectful, "Howdy, Miss Reveille, ma'am," when she is in their presence. The greeting is preferably performed while looking away

Birthday Bash

Most dogs are fortunate if they are thrown a bone on their birthday. But when her big day rolls around each year, Reveille receives more than she could ever imagine or digest. And there's no telling to what lengths future E-2 freshmen will go to honor the First Lady of Texas A&M and top their predecessors in the unit.

Although freshmen in Company E-2 are not even permitted to allow their eyes to linger on Reveille, there's an unwritten rule among the members of the outfit that each new freshman class is expected to surpass the efforts of the previous one in celebrating her birthday. That means the birthday cakes continue to increase in size and ornamentation.

For Reveille VII's second birthday in 2002, each freshman in the E-2 outfit pitched in roughly thirty dollars to purchase a three-tiered wedding cake featuring roses and maroon velvet. The overall price of the cake, which featured the inscription, "Happy Birthday, Miss Reveille, Ma'am," was roughly five hundred dollars.

"We also made a banner that went from stairwell to stairwell in the hallway of the dorm that said, 'Happy Birthday, Miss Reveille, Ma'am,'" said Jerred Crumley, a freshman in 2002–2003. "Then we filled the floor of the hallway with regular balloons and the ceiling with helium-filled balloons and put Christmas lights everywhere. We did this all at like 3:00 or 4:00 A.M. when the upperclassmen were asleep, and they were so impressed with what we did. We also had the singing cadets come and sing "Happy Birthday" to her while we were there, and we wore birthday hats that night when we brought the cake out."

The only items the freshmen in 2002–2003 forgot were plates and forks. But that actually added to the fun. "We forgot the utensils, so the upperclassmen just started grabbing the cake and smashing it in our faces," Crumley recalled. "This huge food fight broke out. Rev didn't get any cake, of course, but it was also the first time she'd ever seen a balloon, and we had those balloons all over the place. She was kicking them around. It was just a lot of fun."

Reveille's birthday is always a big event for members of Company E-2. In 2002, for example, members of the outfit's fresh-man class raised five hundred dollars for a multi-tiered, wedding-style birthday cake that wound up producing quite a food fight. Courtesy Cushing Library

from her and after the freshmen have slammed their backs against a wall in a show of respect for the highest ranking member of the Corps of Cadets. After the greeting, fish are expected to run in another direction from her, so she will not be forced to linger in the presence of a "lowly" fish. According to E-2 legend, several freshmen have leapt out of windows to avoid eye contact with her, and it is common practice for fish to dive under beds, on top of bunks, or into closets to avoid offending her. In fact, for most of the year, freshmen are not even allowed to gaze at all the pictures of present and previ-

ous mascots in the hallways. The only time freshmen are typically permitted to touch Reveille is when they are awarded the "privilege" of providing her a bath.

The rituals of respect obviously have much more to do with A&M's military ties, the class system within the corps, and the protocol of the particular outfit than Reveille's actual preferences. After all, "non-reg" freshmen (those who are not in the corps) seem perfectly acceptable and often quite pleasing to Miss Reveille, ma'am. But in E-2, it's all part of the rite of passage. And any freshman who even ponders the possibility of

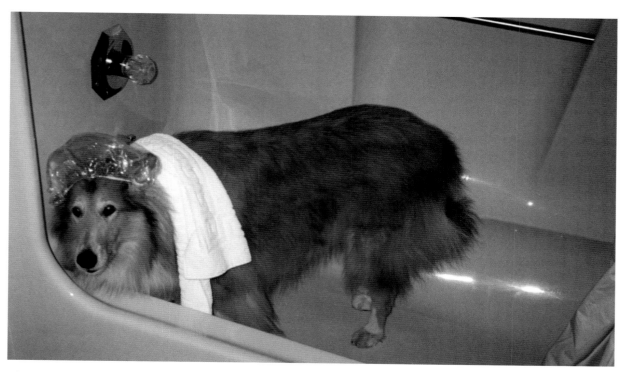

After a long day of meeting, greeting, and posing for pictures, Reveille VI hits the showers. Courtesy Kevin Graham

passing from fish to Mascot Corporal must be prepared to practically major in the "History of Reveille" and minor in push-ups.

Among other things, Mascot Corporal candidates must commit to memory the dates in which each Reveille served, the standard operating procedures regarding her care, and practically every tidbit of Reveille trivia they can pull from the archives of the Cushing Library. They are allowed to make notes while scanning back issues of newspapers dating back to the early 1930s, but they are not permitted to make copies. Candidates also submit papers on Reveille, ranging from the characteristics of the breed to the proper grooming techniques. The nine-week tryout process for Mascot Corporal, which begins before spring break and culminates in a vote of classmates and upperclassmen at parents' weekend, is as much a test of one's ability to handle sleep deprivation as it is a test of knowledge.

"A normal day [in the tryout process] would start by doing our corps stuff in the morning, then we would go to class, go to Cushing Library for research, come back to the dorm for more corps stuff, study a little bit, and then more Rev stuff at night," said Jerred Crumley, the Mascot Corporal for Reveille VII in 2003–2004. "It was like we never slept. I felt like a zombie for nine weeks, as we just wandered around aimlessly. I think the reason they laminate the old articles in the Cushing Library is so when the guys trying out fall asleep, the librarians can easily wipe the drool off all the pages. It's a pretty grueling process, but, without a doubt, it was worth every minute. It's such an honor to care for Reveille and represent this university, as well as all of the other great men who have served in this same role for decades."

The tradition of the Mascot Corporal dates all the way back to Reveille II, the purebred Shetland shepherd that arrived on campus in 1952 as a gift from Mr. and Mrs. Arthur Weinert of Seguin, Texas. At the time of Reveille II's presentation to the school, Weinert, a member of the class of 1900, said he had contemplated presenting a canine mascot to the student body of Texas A&M ever since the original Reveille had died in 1944. In Weinert's way of thinking, a canine mascot at Texas A&M just felt right. He wasn't alone in those sentiments.

DOGS THAT BRIDGED THE GAP

When the first Reveille was laid to rest in 1944, few students could fathom finding a replacement to live up to the standards of the original. But by 1946, the Allied troops had claimed victories in Europe and Japan, and many Aggies were returning to College Station from their wartime duties. It was a celebratory time, a time of new beginnings. Tom Westbrook, a student war veteran from Waco, believed it was also time to move the mascot tradition forward. According to reports in the *Battalion*, Westbrook presented Texas A&M with Rusty, a four-month-old mutt, to continue the tradition of a canine mascot at A&M. In a June 6, 1946, article, the *Bryan Eagle* described Rusty and instructed its readers to "look for a dapper little pup with her hair freshly combed, maroon and white 'T-Aggies' gracing her blanket and a 220-piece band behind her."

In March, 2003, Company E-2 selected Jerred Crumley as the 2003–2004 Mascot Corporal. Reveille VII obviously approves of the selection. Courtesy Jerred Crumley

Despite the press clippings, Rusty apparently wasn't mascot material. Even after great effort and many earnest training attempts by band members and other cadets, Rusty had several significant flaws as a mascot. First, she didn't like crowds; and, even more problematic, she wasn't particularly fond of loud music. When Arkansas came to Kyle Field to play the Aggies in early November of 1946, Rusty was still a no-show; she had not appeared at a single football game. But during the Aggie band's halftime performance that day, Freckles, an energetic cocker spaniel, bounded onto the field to the roar of an approving crowd that had been accustomed to seeing Reveille in a similar mode.

35

Freckles, the frisky cocker spaniel who served as an unofficial mascot between Reveille I and II, endeared herself to Aggieland when in 1946 she joined the Aggie Band during its halftime performance. Courtesy Cushing Library

Only one person in the stadium actually knew who the dog was, but she was an instant hit with the fans. Miss Freckles, as she came to be known, was originally owned by Jimmie Rich, a local businessman and the manager of George's Confectionery. Rich's young child was allergic to dog hair, so he gave the dog to Hal Mullins, a student at A&M and a member of the Aggie band. Despite school polices against personal pets in the dorms, Mullins decided to keep the cocker spaniel in his room, which seemed to be a common practice back in those days.

"Freckles would romp, run, and play as the band practiced marching formations out behind the band dorm—dorm number 11," said Mullins, class of 1948. "Well, the next football game was against Arkansas, and we shut Freckles up in my room, which was number 310, and the band led the corps to Kyle Field. In those days, we seldom kept the dormitory locked, and when someone heard Freckles barking, they let her out and she took off. I suppose like a bloodhound she tracked the band to Kyle Field and joined us for the halftime show as if she was trained to do so."

Taking a page out of Reveille's recipe for instant fame, Freckles was the biggest hit of the day. (The Aggies lost the game, 7-0.) Days after the game, in the November 5, 1946, edition of the *Battalion*, editors printed the headline: "Want a mascot? Vote for Freckles." Below the headline was a call to action that read, "Now, it is up to you, the student body of A&M to decide, to give your word of approval or disapproval of this suggestion. ACTION is needed—IMMEDIATE ACTION—in order to permit Freckles to attend the SMU game this Saturday." The students who voted obviously longed for a canine to rekindle the mystique of Reveille, as Freckles was approved as mascot, 618-3. Soon after, Tillie, a renowned Northgate seamstress, provided Freckles with the first of her Aggie blankets, and the little cocker spaniel made her debut in maroon and white at the 1946 SMU game in Dallas. Although she was never actually noted as an "official mascot," Freckles enjoyed all the privileges of the original Reveille: marching with the band during football games, parades, and corps trips and entering classrooms and the mess hall. "One professor of genetics would lock a student out of class if he was just one minute late," Mullins recalled some fifty-five years later. "But the professor would go to the door and allow Freckles in when she would arrive late and scratch on the classroom door. He even put her name on the roll call list."

In 1948, while presenting graduating ROTC cadets with U.S. Army Reserve commissions, Col. Joe Davis surprised Mullins and everyone else in attendance when he called Freckles to the stage and presented her with a commission certificate as a second lieutenant in the U.S. Army K-9 Corps. But while Freckles ranked as a top dog, she was also a one-man dog. When Mullins graduated in 1948 and reported to Ft. Ord in California, Freckles reported with him. "She loved serving as the mascot for those couple of years," Mullins said, "but she and I were very tight. She wasn't really like the first Reveille, who adopted every boy on campus. Freckles made it pretty clear that she belonged to me."

With Freckles gone in 1948, there was at least some movement among the students to adopt another familiar mutt on campus, Spot. According to various articles in the *Battalion*, the dog was known by many cadets for its lazy ways and its fascination for the football stadium. Unfortunately, Spot would ultimately be known as accident prone. The dog once fell off the top of Kyle Field's single deck and broke both front paws. Spot recovered from the fall but did not survive being run over by a car a short time later.

None of the aforementioned dogs was ever officially designated as the university mascot, although the *Battalion* did use that term in regard to Freckles. In April of 1951, the Corps of Cadets voted in favor of obtaining a new mascot to inherit the official title and the name of "Reveille." The student senate appointed a committee to raise funds for the purchase of a German shepherd, but the funding fell short. On January 12, 1952, Arthur Weinert presented Reveille II and the papers of ownership to Grady L. Smallwood, who as president of the student senate accepted the Shetland shepherd puppy on behalf of the student body. Because of liability issues, Reveille II was not considered to be owned by the university but, rather, by the students.

Upon her arrival, John Henry Pelts built a doghouse that was eventually placed near Duncan Mess Hall. Reveille II quickly made herself at home on campus and began making friends, not all of whom were human. According to the *Battalion* of December 10, 1952, Reveille II gave birth to a litter of ten puppies at the Small Animal Veterinary Clinic. "Reveille and her flock will return home later this week to the band dormitory," Dr. Charles W. Zahn, the administering veterinarian, told the newspaper. "The band paid for the cost of medicine and other expenses, so I guess the pups are going [to the band], too."

Before taking up permanent residence with A Company Quartermaster, the predecessor to Company E-2, Reveille II lived in this doghouse just outside Duncan Mess Hall. Courtesy Cushing Library

Like Reveille I, the second official mascot of Texas A&M was "adopted" by virtually all of the students. But also like the original, Reveille II initially seemed particularly attached to the band and was most often associated with its members. According to Sam Netterville, who would later play an integral part in Reveille II's life, at some point between the end of 1952 and the summer of 1954, Reveille II's doghouse burned down. It was never determined whether the incident was a prank, an accident, or the actions of a rival fan. Regardless, Reveille II apparently became a campus nomad without a home for some time. In fact, she was wandering the campus in the summer of 1954 when Larry Hill, class of '56, found her unattended on the main drill field in front of the Memorial Student Center. She appeared hungry, so Hill took her into the MSC, fed her breakfast, and took her to class with him.

It was Hill, a native of Beaumont, Texas, who first "introduced" Reveille II to Netterville, who also hailed from Beaumont. Since there were still no female students at A&M, Netterville and Hill would frequently make weekend journeys home—especially during the summer—in search of eligible females. It was during one of those trips to Beaumont when Netterville bonded with a female who would rarely leave his side for the next two years. As Netterville hopped behind the wheel of his car, Reveille II requisitioned the front passenger's seat, leaving Hill to the backseat. "That seating arrangement—with Reveille in the front seat—would remain intact until she and I were separated upon my graduation," Netterville recalled. "I even remember one date I had with a woman named Lou Birdwell, now Lou Parris, who came down one weekend from Georgetown. Reveille would not let her sit in the front seat of my car. But Lou loved dogs, and it was not long before Lou and Reveille were both in the front seat. To this day, I believe Reveille really liked Lou, or she would have never shared the front seat."

Reveille II may have been the most protective mascot of the entire line of Revs. Because of the bond, Reveille II lived with Netterville and his roommate, George Stevens—both members of A Company Quartermaster—in dorm 3. That living arrangement unofficially began the ties between the outfit (now E-2) and the mascot that have never been severed. Netterville says he never initially intended to begin the tradition of the "Mascot Company." At the outset, he was concerned

You can practically see the mischief in Reveille II's eyes in this picture taken shortly after her arrival in Aggieland in 1952. Rev II later became the only A&M mascot ever to give birth to puppies, delivering a litter of ten. Courtesy Cushing Library

about the well-being of the university's symbol, but as he looked into those big, brown eyes and grew accustomed to her turned-over and constantly wagging tail, Netterville acknowledges that he quickly fell in love with the feisty but warm-hearted "First Lady." Some would say she was merely panting, but Netterville swears he could see a huge smile on her face. And while some may have considered it a nuisance to share a dorm room with a large dog and another young man, Netterville viewed it as a privilege.

However, with meager means for dog food and other supplies, Netterville decided it was time to seek some financial help in the care of Reveille II. He scheduled an appointment with Pete Hardstean, the head of student activities, to solicit funds for the basic upkeep of the animal. "Pete was very nice but stated that there were no funds for Reveille II because neither the A&M College of Texas nor the State of Texas owned Reveille II due to the liability," Netterville said. "I informed the head of student activities that in that case, A Company Quartermaster owned Reveille II. That day I vowed to myself that A Company Quartermaster would always retain the ownership of Reveille II. I presented to the student senate and requested that a resolution be passed that Reveille would always be cared for and come under the command of A Quartermaster. The resolution was passed."

Without any university funding, Netterville placed waste baskets at the entrances of the mess hall and asked the Corps of Cadets to participate in the upkeep of Reveille II. The cadets supported the idea, pitching pennies, nickels, and dimes into the waste basket. The spare change became the one source of funding for her

dog food and other supplies. And if Netterville was ever short, his stepfather covered the remaining necessities. "My stepdad, C. N. Magee, class of '34, funded a major part of all the costs pertaining to Reveille II," Netterville said. "A Company Quartermaster and I appreciated his assistance more than he could have ever known, God rest his soul."

With Reveille II now under the care and control of A Company Quartermaster, she began truly asserting herself on campus. With Netterville at the other end of her leash, she attended yell practices, marched to meals with her newly adopted outfit, traveled on corps trips, attended numerous classes, and even attended movies and church services. According to Netterville, she was always particularly well-behaved in church, as well as other "quiet times" such as Silver Taps and Aggie Muster. But always the sweet tooth, she would lie on the floor during movies and pick the gum off the bottoms of the seats. Inevitably, she would leave the feature with gum entangled in her white and tan fur.

Reveille II also took great delight in checking the mail at the Memorial Student Center. When Netterville found correspondence in his box, he would first tell her that they had mail, which induced a victory dance of sorts, as she whimpered with delight. She became so excited about the mail that Netterville's mother would send him letters in two envelopes, so he could give Reveille the outside envelope. She would proudly carry it across campus for hours—until the once-dry envelope had practically dissolved in her mouth.

But like the Reveille before her (and even Freckles, for that matter) Reveille II made her biggest mark on

Reveille II, the Shetland shepherd who took great pride in keeping visitors off the field during the Aggie band's halftime performances, earned the "naughty girl of Aggieland" nickname for allegedly biting a referee and an opposing coach.
Courtesy Cushing Library

Did You Say "Parade"?

During the 1950s, Sam Netterville and two of his friends, Larry Hill and Vince Giradina, decided to take Reveille II to see Texas A&M play at Arkansas. Netterville's stepfather, C. N. Magee, financed the trip, and the quartet headed for the Ozarks, not knowing that it was the Razorbacks' homecoming.

Thanks to an Old Ag with a few beers under his belt, Netterville, Reveille, and friends landed a room on the Friday night before the game. Later on Friday, the First Lady and her male companions went to the Pi Phi sorority house on the Arkansas campus to seek dates.

"We were in full uniform—senior boots and all," Netterville recalled. "Some lady came to the door, and I said, 'Ma'am, we are from Texas A&M, and we are looking for dates.' In just a few minutes, we had dates, and the girls loved Reveille. They informed us that the next day was the homecoming parade. Well, we ended up in the homecoming parade. Reveille got us in the parade."

Kyle Field. Many times, in fact, she left marks that could be seen and smelled. Her bathroom pit stops became a source of amusement and considerable wagering among the fans. In the crowd, bets would be placed regarding which yard line Reveille would randomly select upon her entrance into the stadium. Later in her life, the mascot handlers trained her specifically to use yard lines only on the visitors' side of the field.

At one point during the 1955 football season, the commandant of the Corps of Cadets, Col. Joe Davis, instructed Netterville not to let Reveille II loose during the band's halftime performance. Netterville appeared on a local radio program about the yard-line betting. He announced that under orders from the commandant, Rev II would remain leashed at the A&M-Rice game in Houston. As soon as his announcement was made, the switchboard at the station was overloaded with calls of protest. At the game, seventy-two thousand spectators piled into Rice Stadium, with the vast majority of those in attendance being Aggie fans. Technically, Netterville followed his orders, but he had taught Reveille to slip out of her harness. She did just that at halftime, bolting onto the field and performing her ritual to the roar and wagers of the crowd. "It took some smooth talking to get my way out of demerits that next Monday morning," Netterville said.

While Reveille II caused plenty of laughs by doing her business on the field, she also possessed a businesslike approach when she was unleashed onto the playing surface. In her own mind, Reveille II had a specific role to play at halftime. From the time she was first brought to campus in 1952 until the day she died—August 23, 1966—Reveille II had a love affair with the

Caught up in the excitement of a Saturday afternoon football game in the fall, Reveille IV lets the Rice Owls' mascot know who rules the sideline in the old Southwest Conference.
Courtesy Cushing Library

Whether she is on the road for work-related travel or on a dirt road in the country, Reveille adapts quickly to her unusual lifestyle. Courtesy Jerred Crumley

Farm Girl

Aside from the original Reveille, all of the following A&M mascots—one Shetland shepherd and five American collies—have been at home on the farm because of their herding instincts.

But perhaps Reveille II was the most comfortable of all on the open range. In the summer of 1962, Mascot Corporal Andrew Salge took Rev II home with him and turned her loose on the cattle at his parents' farm. She was such a natural and so effective on the farm that Salge practically was forced to wrestle her from his father at the end of the summer.

"My dad was semi-retired, but he would graze these small patches on our farm, which contained a pretty good number of cattle," Salge recalled. "He would graze them every day, and one day he said, 'Well, Rev, let's go get the cows.' He walked down to the end of the patch with her, and the cows were kind of used to it, but they weren't used to that large of a dog. My dad used to keep rat terriers, and Reveille got their attention right away. He made the rounds with her, got behind the cattle and pushed them out, and the next day, dad did it again. He said, 'Rev, let's go get the cows.' He took about two steps toward the electric fence, and Rev just took off on her own. She went down and circled the herd and pushed them out and dad just stood there with his mouth open. He came home that evening and said, 'That's a pretty darn impressive dog. Can I keep her here on the farm to work cattle?' I said, 'Well, if you try to keep her you might gain a dog and lose a son. The school's answer is going to be "no."'"

Aggie band. She belonged to Company E-2, but the band was always her special pet project. She marched with them on the field; her ears perked when the band played; and she obviously fancied herself as their half-time performance protector. Especially as she aged, Reveille would circle the field, making sure anyone not affiliated with the band stayed on the sideline. She felt quite comfortable weaving in and out of the band's precision movements, but she was not about to allow anything else to interfere with the "pulse of Aggieland." She allegedly bit an official once—perhaps because he tried to enter the field too early. A TCU assistant coach also accused her of biting him, forcing school officials to muzzle the spirited mascot occasionally.

"She was an extremely intelligent dog," said Andrew Salge, the Mascot Corporal for Reveille II in 1963–64. "It used to amaze me that when we would turn her loose with the band at halftime, she seemed to know their formations, never tripping a band member or causing a misstep. She believed that she owned that field, and she had pure disdain for the striped shirts of officials until her dying day. Toward the end of the halftime performances, the sideline officials would invariably walk across the end zone to their positions, and she'd zero

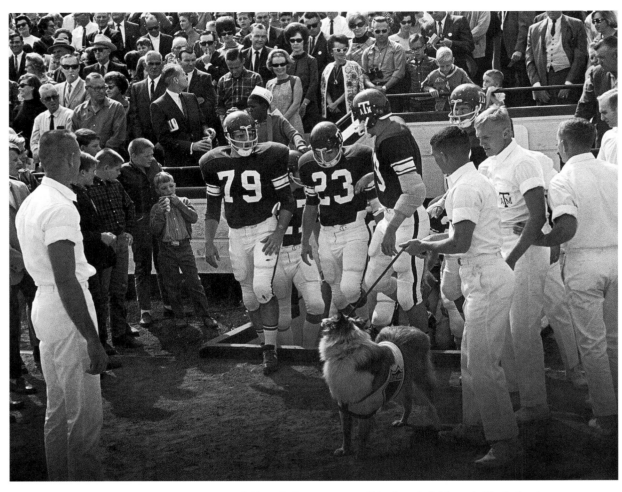

Reveille III prepares to lead the Aggies onto the field in the late 1960s as yell leader Neal Adams holds the leash.
Courtesy Neal Adams

in on them. She'd run up to the edge of that sideline marker or that end zone marker and she'd be bouncing and barking and raising cain. She never did go outside the boundaries and bite them again. But . . . she had to wear a muzzle, and I think she always resented the officials because they caused her to wear a muzzle."

By the time Salge inherited her in 1963–64, Reveille's role with Company E-2 had been cemented, and the tradition of an annual Mascot Corporal had become an accepted practice. According to E-2's records, the first official Mascot Corporal was Jackie Shelton in 1959–60. But the groundwork had undeniably been laid by Calvin Samuel Netterville, who embraced the Shetland shepherd first with concerned respect and later with deep-seated warmth and love. When Netterville became the commanding officer of A Company Quartermaster in 1955–56, his role with Rev began to change somewhat, as he began assigning freshmen and sophomores some of the day-to-day responsibilities of her care, health, and training—a change that would eventually lead to the evolution of underclassmen as Mascot Corporals. She didn't initially take kindly to this new set of circumstances, but, like any good cadet, she accepted the arrangement.

"There's no doubt in my mind that she understood that she had a role to play, a role that was bigger than that of a typical dog," Netterville said. "She was a brilliant dog and truly a loyal and loving friend. I don't really know what would have happened to her if Larry Hill had not found her that day in the summer of 1954. But I know I am very proud to have played a role in the legacy of this tradition that has evolved into E-2 being the Mascot Company. And I feel very fortunate to have bonded with that very special little lady."

Indeed, Reveille II was a special lady, albeit a feisty, protective, and mischievous one. She was the second part of a series, but without a doubt, she lived up to the title as the "First Lady of Aggieland."

CHAPTER 3

Collie Station

AGGIELAND'S BREED OF CHOICE

DR. E. W. ELLETT, the associate professor of veterinary medicine and surgery at Texas A&M, spoke with a compassionate, sympathetic tone that indicated his understanding of Reveille II's place in the hearts of the student body. He did not, however, provide any false hopes. In no uncertain terms, Ellett clearly affirmed what many of the students had come to fear as they watched Reveille slow down with age. At fourteen—the equivalent of more than one hundred years old for humans—Rev II was on the verge of death. It was February of 1966, her kidneys were failing, and Ellett began to prepare the student body for the inevitable uremic poisoning that would likely take her life at any moment. Ellett didn't expect her to recover from the February health crisis, telling the *Battalion,* "Her life expectancy is very short. But we just don't give up on old Reveille very easily."

She had never given anyone reason to give up on her. After all, her kidney troubles began in 1956, as a seizure destroyed a large amount of the organ's tissue. She battled the condition for a decade, symbolically representing a university that prided itself on its war heroes with their uncommon valor and never-say-die attitude. She was a lover, but she was also a warrior. To the surprise of her doctors, Reveille II survived the February health problems and was released from the clinic to her caretakers in Company E-2 by early March. Her brush with death did stir the debate and hasten the need to find a replacement for Reveille II. In fact, such discussions began as early as the fall of 1965, as Rev II was slowed by a calcium deposit on the ball joint of her left rear hip.

In late October of 1965, the student newspaper voiced its opinion on the subject, nominating Ranger

Reveille makes herself at home anywhere on campus. Here, she takes a moment's rest on the university president's front lawn. Photo by Allen Pearson, courtesy Texas A&M University Relations

Ranger, the mischievous bulldog owned by former A&M president James Earl Rudder, often carried a message on his side as students penned or painted memos on him. But Ranger's favorite pastime was hitchhiking. Courtesy Cushing Library

as the next canine mascot of the university. It was an absurd suggestion to some, a logical one to others. Ranger—known affectionately to many friends on campus as "Earl"—was the loveable, laughable bulldog owned by university president James Earl Rudder. The dog was named in honor of the famous Second Ranger Battalion, which, under Rudder's command, had courageously stormed the beach at Pointe du Hoc during the D-Day invasion in World War II. Under constant fire, Rudder's Rangers scaled one-hundred-foot cliffs to reach and destroy German gun batteries. In that context, the name "Ranger" symbolized bravery, commitment, and victory. But the dog that bore the Ranger name on campus was considered more of a slobbering sideshow than a symbol of excellence.

Don't misunderstand. Ranger was certainly beloved on the Texas A&M campus, and he was definitely the unofficial mascot of Aggieland. But he was more of a loveable misfit than a respected or adored mascot. The first Ranger owned by the Rudder family had died prior to Rudder's moving to College Station to become the sixteenth president of the university in the summer of 1959. So it was Ranger II that made his debut on the A&M campus, and the bulldog certainly made a lasting impression on all the cadets he encountered. According to various published reports and numerous personal accounts, Ranger was a walking, barking, four-legged billboard in the politically charged 1960s. Whether his fine fur was marked by felt-tip pen or a message had been fastened to his side, Ranger usually carried a memorandum on his midsection—ranging from "Beat the hell outta" the team that was next on Texas A&M's schedule to "Go home Maggies," a reference to the new female students whom President Rudder had played a vital role in admitting. Whether a particular message was washed off immediately or allowed to wear off was probably determined by Rudder's particular stance on the matter.

Ranger, however, was also famous on campus for many other memorable moments and unique personality traits. He once crashed the Fish Ball, turning up underneath a young woman's billowing, formal gown. He also filled in once for a sick Reveille at a home game and, upon being unleashed, tripped a half-dozen band members during the halftime performance, attacked the bass drummer, and assaulted the University of Houston's costumed cougar mascot. But perhaps his favorite pastime—the activity that truly produced joyous yelps in his monstrous jowls—was hitchhiking. Ranger loved to chase cars, hurtling his compact frame toward the front wheel of an oncoming car, believing always that the driver would slam on his brakes at the appropriate time. If the driver could remove his head from the windshield or dashboard and was willing to open the door, Ranger was always a willing and excited passenger. While many dogs enjoy chasing cars, Ranger's mission was not necessarily the pursuit but, rather, the passenger seat. The Rudders once attempted to curtail his carjacking by tying him up on the president's lawn, but Ranger reacted like a toddler whose favorite toy had just been trashed. He settled in the back of his doghouse and sulked, catching a skin disease after his extended stay indoors. Realizing Ranger would never be a happily confined canine, the Rudders unchained him, allowing him to romp free and wreak roadside havoc once again.

"I remember Reveille being on the field during games, but Ranger was the one always roaming the campus," said Edd Hargett, who led the Aggies to the 1967 Southwest Conference championship and was a two-time All-SWC quarterback. "I vividly recall that Ranger would come into class and lay down on the floor and go to sleep. But most of all, I remember he would run around in front of your car until you would be forced to stop. Then he would want you to open your car door for him to get in. He just wanted to go for a ride. Reveille was our school mascot, but Ranger was kind of the fun-loving prankster that was always interacting with the students. He wasn't real pretty to look at, but he had some serious personality, grunting, scratching, drooling, and whatever else. He was kind of our running joke."

In some circles, Ranger may have been even more popular than Reveille, but Ranger was the wrong choice as A&M's official mascot, for a variety of reasons. First, he was, well, a he. The first two Reveilles had been female, and as legend has it at A&M, if something is done twice it is considered a tradition. There were also numerous schools—Georgia, Butler, the Citadel, Drake, Fresno State, Gonzaga, Louisiana Tech, Mississippi State, Samford, South Carolina State, and Yale, to name a few—that already possessed a bulldog mascot. A place as distinctive as Texas A&M needed a distinctive dog. The Aggies, already the object of countless jokes throughout the state and region, probably didn't need a mascot that was often viewed as a joke even on their own campus, either. The students decided the school needed a breed that commanded some respect. It was also preferred that, whatever the breed,

Posed and poised for her new role, Reveille VI has the look of an All-American girl. Courtesy Texas A&M Sports Information

The queen surveys her new palace. Reveille IV takes a walk in front of the Academic Building on campus as her Mascot Corporal, Bob Vanderberry, provides free reign. Courtesy Cushing Library

the mascot should come from within the Aggie family, adding maroon ties to the lineage of the mascot.

Reveille I picked A&M, while Reveille II was donated by an Aggie family. Aggies were open to newcomers, but those with A&M ties enjoyed a special priority on the growing campus. So, when Randy and

Steve Andes, twin brothers and students at A&M from Alaska, first learned that Reveille II was nearing retirement, they placed a call to their parents. The brothers believed their parents, Mr. and Mrs. Joseph Husa, could provide a collie puppy that would satisfy the requirements and expectations of the A&M faithful on

Reveille and Company E-2 have been joined at the leash since the 1950s. Here, Reveille III appears to be inspecting some senior boots. Courtesy Cushing Library

many fronts. No other major university possessed an American collie as its mascot, which certainly appealed to the distinctive desires of the Aggies. The popularity of Lassie added instant credibility to the breed, and the predominant coloring of the canine—golden brown and white—bore a resemblance to the beloved Reveille II. The breed even provided a unique combination of the Aggie image—the poise, polish, and prestige of a cadet at final review and the rugged, working-class dog mentality of a ranch hand. In fact, the natural herding instincts of the breed seemed to make her a natural candidate as the mascot of the 12th Man.

"Collies were originally bred to be social, herding animals," said Dr. Cindi Bossart. "So when Reveille sees all these people running around on the field or on the court, her natural instinct is to put everything in order. That's a big reason why you always see her barking on the sidelines. She wants the world that she is surrounded by to be in order. She literally wants to be the 12th Man on the field, rounding up the players. I believe if she was enabled to do what she wanted to do that she would have those football players in a circle in a matter of seconds. The whole idea with having a collie as the mascot epitomizes the bravery, loyalty, and intelligence Texas A&M represents. I'm a veterinarian who was a cheerleader at Georgia Tech and then went to the University of Pennsylvania. But the spirit, camaraderie, loyalty, and bond at A&M are really something special. That goes hand in hand with the collie, making Reveille, in my opinion, the perfect mascot for Texas A&M."

The student body in 1966 obviously shared similar sentiments. The Andes twins firmed up the arrange-

Queen Collie

Not only is an American collie the queen of Texas A&M, but all collies today have a connection to the queen, as Queen Victoria saved the collies from obscurity on the farm in the early 1860s.

Collies started out as lowly working dogs, cherished only by the farmers who relied on their hardworking canine companions to tend their flocks of sheep. The original collies were closer to the size and shape of border collies, not the large, heavy-coated breed we know today. The collies of yesteryear were also predominantly black. Since they were bred for their herding abilities rather than looks, they varied greatly in appearance.

The dogs that worked the rough terrain of Scotland's hill country and endured its cold, blustery winters were hardy and independent, able to work far from their masters. They needed to be both quick to respond to commands and able to solve problems on their own, for the lives of the sheep often depended on the response and decisions of the dogs. Intelligence, independence, and responsiveness are the characteristics that continue to make them popular generations after most collies have ceased to work with sheep and shepherds.

On a visit to Scotland in 1860, Queen Victoria fell in love with the good looks and gentle personalities of the collies and began the first collie fad. Soon the dogs were being shown and bred more for good looks than for working ability.

Reveille III was the first American collie in the line of mascots and arrived on campus prior to the death of Rev II.
Courtesy Cushing Library

ments with the student senate even before Reveille III was born, and at eight weeks old, the floppy-eared, sable ball of fluff made the flight from Fairbanks, Alaska, to College Station, Texas. To the delight of the students and the surprise of the veterinarians, Reveille II lived into the summer, overseeing the arrival of the new mascot. Reveille II's condition began to worsen after the arrival of the puppy. In her final days, Rev II's arthritis rendered her unable to stand up on her own power, and on August 23, she was put to sleep at the Small Animal Clinic. "We couldn't see putting her through a long course of treatment and felt this would be the best and most humane thing to do," Dr. Ellett said at the time.

While the students, especially those in Company E-2, mourned the death of the old mascot, the transition was made considerably easier with the arrival of Reveille III, a frolicking, frisky pup with a nose for mischief. Rev III's attendance even lightened the solemn tone of the memorial service and burial of Reveille II, which was attended by more than three thousand A&M students, fans, and well-wishers. While the ceremony was somber, it was difficult to remain glum, as Reveille III constantly tugged at the new blanket that adorned her torso, barked at photographers, pawed at the air, nipped at her leash, and finally lay down in utter boredom. In almost all aspects, she was a typically playful, sharp-toothed, gnawing puppy. She enjoyed playing with the orange Frisbee (it was that color, according to several E-2 members, to develop her killer instinct regarding all things orange), chewing on boots, and hiding her handler's belts and spurs that were within her reach. But as she grew, it didn't take long for her to

Reveille III proved her intelligence with her ability to drink out of the dorm water fountain, pushing the button herself and lapping up the water. She usually left a slobbery reminder of her trick, but as the highest-ranking member of the Corps of Cadets, she didn't need to apologize. Courtesy Thomas Rideout

discover that she enjoyed special privileges and pardons that most dogs do not receive.

"Reveille III had this underbite," said Col. Jake Betty, the Mascot Corporal in 1970–71 and now a cadet training officer in the office of the Commandant of the Corps. "At that time, we had the stand-up-type water fountains in the hallway [of the dormitory]. Rev III had learned that she could jump up on the water fountain, put her paw on the button, and drink out of the water fountain. Normally, if we had been outside on a run or something, she would come inside and head to the water fountain, just standing up there drinking out of it. With that underbite, it was easier for her to lap up the water doing that. Personally—this may sound bad— I allowed her to do it because there would be plenty of dog slobber all over the water fountain. The upper classmen would come in after her, griping and whining about all this damn dog slobber all over the water fountain. But since it was Rev, no one ever did anything. I took some joy out of that."

So did Reveille, who loved lapping up the water and the attention from the adoring masses in College Station. With her long nose, flowing coat, and perked ears, Reveille III was, to that point, probably the prettiest mascot ever to grace the A&M campus. This seemed appropriate since the campus itself was becoming much prettier during her tenure, with the admission of female students. In fact, the Alaskan-born collie's coat was so full that it took her several years to adjust fully to the dramatic difference in the climate in College Station. Constant grooming and the natural acclimation over time eventually thinned her coat somewhat, but she was always a lushly furred beauty.

According to several of her handlers, however, Rev III was probably not the sharpest tool in the shed. Loveable, yes. Loyal, absolutely. Playful, warm-hearted, and even tempered, without a doubt. But compared to her predecessors, Reveille III was a little slow when it came to learning new things. Her dim-witted nature probably contributed to the end of the tradition of Reveille marching—or at least performing in an impromptu manner—with the band at halftime of football games. Again and again, handlers and Company E-2 members attempted to coax her onto the field with the band, offering her treats, encouragement, and praise. They even took her to band practices, hoping familiarity might entice her onto the field. But nothing worked.

"She simply couldn't figure out what we were trying to get her to do," said Thomas Rideout, the Mascot Corporal for Rev III in 1969–70. "To put it mildly, she was more of a lover than a thinker. I have very fond memories of her, but not because of her intelligence. I remember her because she loved to play, and, for the most part, she had a real gentle, kind nature."

Except on game days. It may have been the roar of the crowd and the excitement of the atmosphere. It could have been her herding instincts, propelling her to create order out of chaos. Or perhaps it was an innate, 12th Man intuition. Whatever the case, Reveille III often changed from mild-mannered canine into an aggressive beast when the Aggies took the fields or courts. In stark contrast to her typical personality, Reveille III would begin nipping and biting the yell leaders as soon as they led her onto the field. She despised costumed mascots, loved to bark in the direction of opposing teams, and even played a large role in a sig-

Connecticut Fan Writes to "Rev" (reprinted from the October 15, 1969, edition of the Battalion)

Texas A&M's mascot, Reveille, is truly a distinguished celebrity. Along with being the only school mascot in the Southwest Conference that has never been stolen, she has drawn acclaim from Aggies in Kyle Field, beer cans and rocks from Tiger Stadium, crowds in Baton Rouge, and now she even has an admirer in Stamford, Conn.

The following letter was addressed to Reveille, Texas A&M University, College Station, Texas:

Dear Reveille,
My father was an Aggie. When I was a little girl he told me all about you and the other Reveilles. Yesterday we went to see you and the Aggies play Army at West Point. You are one of the most prettiest dogs I have seen. If you have a picture of yourself, could you please send it to me so I could hang it on my bulletin board? We will always cheer for you and the Aggies.

Your friend,
Shannon Gleason

P.S. Gig 'em, Aggies

The letter was forwarded to Company E-2, the outfit that guards and cares for "Miss Reveille Ma'am" and then to Rev's handler, Mascot Corporal Robert Snedden, a sophomore from Ennis.

"I was really surprised," Snedden said, "and glad that someone cared that much about Rev to go to that much trouble."

"I wrote her a letter," Snedden added, "thanking her for expressing an interest in Rev and told her that a picture would be in the mail soon."

So now the Aggie mascot has a female fan to add to her large collection of male admirers.

Company E-2 hopes Shannon enjoys the picture and invites her down to visit Reveille anytime.

nificant basketball victory over Arkansas in the early 1970s. Former A&M basketball coach Shelby Metcalf, who produced more wins than any other coach in the history of the Southwest Conference, credits Reveille III with the single best defensive game in the history of Aggie basketball. "Arkansas's leading scorer came into G. Rollie White [Coliseum] on a hot streak," Metcalf recalled. "This kid from Arkansas ran along the side [of the court] early in the game. I don't know if he said something to Reveille, slapped at her, or what, but she nipped him right in the butt while he was playing. For the rest of the game, every time that boy would get the

Children may have limited attention spans regarding many other A&M traditions, but Reveille has captivated kids since the first Rev arrived on campus in the early 1930s. Here, Reveille IV and Mascot Corporal Jeff Gruetzmacker pose with a young girl. Courtesy Jeff Gruetzmacker

ball, Reveille would bark. He missed shot after shot. I really think he was scared of Reveille, or at least distracted by her. She would bark, and man, he would throw up some wild shots. Reveille just shut down Arkansas's leading scorer. That's the only time Reveille had ever done that, so she must have been provoked. But she obviously had some spunk, passion, and personality."

All of the collies who have served as Texas A&M's mascots since then have certainly exhibited those same traits. And unlike Reveille III, who may have been a bit slow in her mental capacities, the successors in the mascot lineage at A&M have often bordered on brilliant.

While many dogs can recognize past care providers from years ago, Reveille VI once spotted a single face in a crowd of some forty thousand spectators. With the Aggie football team opening the 1999 season on the road against Louisiana Tech, Rev VI spotted a familiar person in the A&M section and repeatedly pulled on Mascot Corporal Kevin Graham to allow her to move closer to the stands at Shreveport's Independence Stadium. When curiosity finally overcame him, Graham relented, allowing Reveille to move closer to the fans. Upon reaching the edge of the stands, Reveille put her paws on top of the chain-linked fence as a young woman came to greet her. Graham introduced

Before the arrival of the Aggie Dance Team, Reveille provided most of the timeout and halftime entertainment at basketball games by catching her Frisbee. Courtesy Texas A&M Sports Information

himself to the young woman, who happened to be the sister of Jim Lively—the Mascot Corporal six years earlier. "Rev was just [nine] months old when she lived at Jim Lively's house for just three months during the summer," Graham said. "Rev remembered Lively's sister six years later and even picked her out of the crowd. I went, 'Wow, these are really clever dogs.' But that's the thing about Rev VI and, for that matter, all of the collie mascots. They remember Mascot Corporals and guys in the unit for as long as they live. That's why it is so fun to go back and see her."

Reveilles III, IV, VI, and VII were all uncanny in their canine sixth senses. But perhaps the mascot that most personified the image of being more than just a dog was Reveille V, who was truly the epitome of grace with a collar. Rev V, who served as the mascot from 1984 to 1994, was a little different from other dogs right from the start. That, in fact, was the reason she was chosen as the mascot. Company E-2 cadets visited puppies in Del Rio, San Antonio, and Houston before settling on a twelve-week-old American collie from Del Rio. The cadets considered about fifteen American collies, several other puppies of different breeds, and even inquired about selecting a puppy from an animal shelter—an idea promoted by several people connected with the Humane Society and one that would more similarly model the origins of the first mascot. But the risk of taking any dog from a shelter is that there is often no way of determining potentially inherited health problems from the parents. Reveille V's bloodlines, however, appeared to be healthy and strong. She also seemed to be the most developed and intelligent puppy the cadets encountered in their statewide search. Un-

like Reveilles II, III, and IV, she didn't come from an Aggie family, but she did come from an A&M fan, Raymond Carrell, who bred collies as a hobby in Del Rio. After reading about Reveille IV's retirement, Carrell contacted an Aggie friend to gauge the school's interest in one of his puppies. Rev V was one of a kind from her first breath—the only female in a litter of four pups—and Carrell instantly named her "Maybe," in reference to her potential as the next A&M mascot.

She became "Definitely" after the cadets first met her. She displayed an alertness the other puppies did not. After surviving an early battle with parvo, an often-fatal viral infection that causes a loss of fluids and electrolytes from the intestinal tract, Reveille V quickly learned and mastered the intricacies of Aggieland. She seemed to embrace the culture of her new surroundings eagerly. She was not, for example, an idle barker. Rev V's bark had a purpose, as she displayed to various reporters and impressed observers over the years. Handlers could excitedly bellow out ordinary words or names in her presence, and Rev V would remain unfazed. For example, spelling out the name "J-E-F-F"—even if it was performed in yell leader tenor and style—would not produce any response. But if anyone in her presence began spelling out "A-G-G-I-E-S," Reveille V would begin enthusiastic and purposeful barking by the second "G" in the cadence. "She was really a brilliant dog, the smartest dog I have ever been around in all my life," said Greg Riels, Reveille V's handler in 1991–92. "So much so, that she really seemed much more like a lady than a dog."

An extremely opinionated, protective, sensitive, and loyal lady, to be exact. Her nature showed especially during the annual changing of the Mascot Corporal. The

Former Mascot Corporal and yell leader Kevin Graham takes Reveille VI across the field during a game at Kyle Field. Courtesy 12th Man Foundation

Reveille V's bark usually had a purpose, as she seemed to know the difference between normal yelling and Aggie yells. Courtesy Texas A&M Sports Information

change creates a difficult transition period for each of the Reveilles. From the mascot's perspective, it is almost like being deserted by a master every 365 days. It's not a complete abandonment, as the Mascot Corporal is only a sophomore and can still interact regularly with Reveille during his final two years in school, which eases the transition on both the human and the collie. The changing of the guard still makes for difficult adjustments for Reveille, though, especially since the new Mascot Corporal has no previously existing bond with her. Except for providing the occasional bath, he has spent his entire first year ducking for cover whenever she has been in his presence. The transition was especially difficult for Reveille V, who seemed rather offended that anyone would ever relinquish control of her leash. She was not initially receptive to her new handlers, and they needed to prove themselves to her before she warmed up to them. Her mannerisms toward new Mascot Corporals made for some interesting nights in her new dorm room. During her first week with Jeff Heath in 1992, for example, Reveille hopped onto his bed as he stayed up late studying. Lying on her side, she placed her head on the pillow, turned her back to Heath, and curled her paws underneath her, nudging her nose and tummy as close to the wall as possible. When Heath finally went to sleep, he slept on the outside of the bed, with Reveille between him and the wall. But Heath soon discovered he was being pushed out of the bed. "Slowly and purposely, she proceeded to just kind of stretch her legs out, pushing against the wall," Heath recalled. "At one point when I woke up in the middle of the night, I was almost on the floor because she was pushing me out. She didn't re-

ally like me very much those first couple of weeks, but it was fun getting to know her and, of course, her getting to know me. Once we bonded, though, it was a really special relationship. She always knew she was very special, and I don't think she ever believed she was a dog."

Probably not. One of the trademarks of most of the collie mascots has been catching a Frisbee. In fact, Reveille running down a flying Frisbee was often the halftime entertainment at Aggie basketball games in G. Rollie White Coliseum. Rev III was good at it; Rev IV mastered the art. But to Rev V, catching a Frisbee apparently was too dog-like for her fancy and far beneath her ladylike demeanor. Various handlers attempted to train her to catch the flying disc, but she showed no interest whatsoever. She would even allow the Frisbee to hit her in the nose, as if to prove a point. But as much as she despised the Frisbee, she possessed an even stronger disdain for baths. Providing Reveille V with a bath was much like stepping into the ring with a world-class wrestler. She loathed being wet and—to prove another point—she once went nearly three days during a particularly long rainy spell without going to the bathroom. Rick Holcomb, the Mascot Corporal in 1986–87, begged, pleaded, and attempted to trick her into the rain, but Rev V would rather hold it than dampen her pristine coat. And to Reveille V, the only duty worthy of venturing into the rain was standing on the sidelines for an Aggie football game. That was mandatory; using the bathroom was not.

She didn't play like other dogs. Perhaps the only things she truly enjoyed retrieving were the erasers in classrooms. As a professor spoke, she would covertly

Tradition has it that if Rev barks in class, the professor is supposed to give the students a walk. In fact, some professors—after a long night—have encouraged Mascot Corporals to make Reveille bark so that they have an excuse for giving the class a walk. Usually, though, Rev uses class time to catch up on her beauty sleep, as Rev V does here. Courtesy Cushing Library

slip to the chalkboard or dry-erase board, lift the eraser from the tray, and casually deliver it to one of the students in class. She didn't act or beg like other dogs, either. And she certainly didn't want to be seen as a dog when she was eating. While living in the dorm,

Reveille V would wait until the lights were out before she would ever meander toward her food bowl. Even in retirement, she was mindful of her privacy, waiting until her foster parents, Joe and Carrie West, would leave the room before she began to eat.

66

The first night she arrived she also taught the Wests and their other animals who pulled rank in her new home. Upon her official retirement on November 25, 1993, the West family drove to campus to pick up Reveille. Joe West, a former Aggie yell leader and retired veterinarian, accepted her leash from Company E-2 and proceeded to escort Reveille to his vehicle. But Reveille would not budge, at least not until West flashed back to his old Air Force days and realized that, as the highest-ranking member of the Corps of Cadets, Reveille V would only walk on his right side. "I thought, 'Oh, sure. Five stars,'" West recalled. "I used to walk on the left side of generals when I was in the Air Force. I got the point right away."

The Wests' family pets were next on Rev's lesson plan for the evening. The Wests owned five other animals—two male dogs and three cats—when Reveille V came into their College Station home. Upon entering her new home for the first time, Rev caught a glimpse of one of the cats, "Skeezs," and instantly bolted for the feline. The shocked cat made a beeline for the backyard, burst through the screen door, crossed the yard, and scurried up and over the back fence as Reveille pursued. "Rev came back into the living room," West said, "looked at us, looked around the room, and seemed to say, 'Where are the other animals? I've got something to say to them, too.' We had five companion animals at that time, and Rev took exactly one second to establish that she was numero uno in the house.... Rev wouldn't roughhouse with other animals, except when Rev VI would come over. Then Rev V was like a different dog. They had that kind of mother-daughter relationship, and they would play together and just love

Grooming Reveille is a daily chore that can take up to an hour to brush out her thick undercoat. April West, daughter of veterinarian and retirement caretaker Joe West, holds a handful of Reveille V's former coat. Courtesy Joe West

Two "First Ladies," Reveille V and VI, pose together regally. Courtesy Texas A&M Sports Information

Who needs a date if you are escorted by the top dog? Reveille V, shown here with her blanket and mum, is the star attraction of any event she attends at Texas A&M. Courtesy Texas A&M Sports Information

the time together. Of course, they both considered themselves royalty. They would chase each other around the oak tree in our front yard until Rev V was absolutely exhausted. She would lie flat here in the living room for hours after those visits."

Reveille V's personality and demeanor cemented the permanent place American collies will likely always enjoy at Texas A&M. Rev III was a loveable, playful, water fountain-lapping trailblazer of collies in College Station; Rev IV was the sweet-natured, intelligent, Frisbee-catching machine who increased the expectations of future collies; and Rev V was the regal darling of the campus who so perfectly fit the description as "The First Lady of Aggieland." With her expressions, dignity, and grace, Rev V probably ruined the chances of any other breed earning a spot as the mascot of Texas A&M.

That's not to say that another breed might not make a more logical choice than the American collie because of the conditions in which Reveille is placed. First of all, College Station is practically the home of the heat index, with temperatures often soaring into triple digits during early home football games. Add in the intense humidity, and a breed with a thinner coat makes a certain amount of sense. Other breeds may also be less susceptible to the intense noise levels that are often produced at Kyle Field, which now can seat more than eighty-seven thousand fans—a far cry from the seating capacity Reveille III first experienced as the new mascot in 1966. And critics of a purebred collie as the A&M mascot often cite the medical records of the past. Reveille III was diagnosed with pancreatic disease in 1973, two years before she died

Mom, I'm Bringing Home a Girl for the Summer

Jeff Gruetzmacker was the first member of his family to attend college. He didn't know much about Texas A&M when he arrived in College Station in the late 1970s, and he knew even less about the Corps of Cadets, Company E-2, and the university's mascot.

But as his freshman year in Company E-2 progressed, Gruetzmacker was captivated by the spirit of Aggieland and mesmerized by the thought of being the Mascot Corporal. He never told his parents that he was seeking the role as Rev's handler, and he didn't think he had much of a chance. But when Gruetzmacker was selected as the 1977–78 Mascot Corporal for Rev IV, he figured it was about time to let his parent in on his new shadow.

"I lucked into E-2, and I must have stumbled into being the Mascot Corporal," Gruetzmacker said. "I got picked to be the Mascot Corporal, and it was at that time that I told my mom and dad, 'Hey, I'm bringing this collie home with me for the summer.' I just kind of sprung it on them. They were okay with that, but then I added to it, saying, 'Although she's a big dog, she's not really an outside dog. She's gonna be in the house, and the thing about Reveille is that she can go everywhere she wants.' Well, that was true in the dorm, but that wasn't exactly true in my mom's house. She might have been A&M's mascot, but it was my mother's house."

Texas A&M's nationally renowned vet school provides the best health care imagin-able for Reveille. Here, Rev V waits for her checkup at the Small Animal Clinic.
Courtesy Joe West

Reveille never forgets her handlers. Here, Rev VI gives a kiss to her former Mascot Corporal, Jeff Bailey, as Craig Serold accompanies her to an Aggie Moms' Club meeting. Courtesy Jeff Bailey

as a result of the ailment. Reveille IV endured a seizure in the early 1980s, suffered from a number of arthritis issues, and developed tumors on her eyelids later in life. Rev V had a long history of gastrointestinal problems, and Reveille VI began having the first of her numerous epileptic seizures during the Aggies' 1995 Alamo Bowl victory over Michigan—when she was only two years old.

For the most part, though, the health threats the collies face seem less of an issue in light of the lifespan of the A&M mascots. According to Dr. Claudia Barton, an A&M veterinarian and the primary medical provider to Reveille, the average life expectancy of a collie is ten to twelve years. Reveille III died just short of her tenth birthday, while Reveille IV died a month shy of her fourteenth birthday. Rev V was euthanized two months shy of turning fifteen. The extraordinary medical attention the mascots have received from A&M's Small Animal Clinic has certainly prolonged the lives of several Revs, and the veterinary expertise used in the selection of Reveille VII would have diagnosed the epilepsy in the family bloodlines of Reveille VI. Moving forward, Dr. Barton believes that with continuing veterinary input during the selection process, A&M officials and Company E-2 members can at least be assured of finding American collies with pure, healthy, and well-documented bloodlines, reducing the possibility of adopting a genetically flawed puppy. Even the heat index issue has been addressed, as Reveille VII was provided with a cool pad to rest on during breaks at particularly hot games.

So, for the foreseeable future, it appears Reveille will remain an American collie. That's not a slight to the mutt (Rev I) or the Shetland shepherd (Rev II) that began the legacy. But as five consecutive A&M mascots have proven, it's difficult for many Aggies to even envision replacing the combined qualities—beauty, grace, intelligence, playfulness, and friendliness—that collies possess. As a group, they have etched an indelible place in the history of Texas A&M and into the hearts of Aggieland. Perhaps another breed could have done the same, but the sable American collie has become about as identified with Texas A&M as maroon and white athletic uniforms and khaki attire in the corps.

"There's just something very captivating and charismatic about the collie," said Jordan Caddick, the Mascot Corporal for Reveille VII in 2002–2003. "And when you combine the allure of the collie with the aura of Texas A&M, I think you have the perfect match."

CHAPTER 4

Dog Gone

THEFT PRODUCES RISE IN POPULARITY

A BITTER, HOWLING north wind swirled outside Jim Lively's north Dallas home before daybreak on December 26, 1993, plummeting the temperature into the low 20s. But even if Lively had been sleeping on the frost-covered front lawn, he could not have experienced a more piercing chill than the one that shot through every fiber of his body when he awoke to two of the cruelest words he'd heard in his young life. At approximately 5:50 on the morning after Christmas, Lively's father, Fred, opened the back door to allow four-month-old Reveille VI into the fenced backyard for a potty break. After pouring himself a cup of coffee, Fred Lively opened the back door again, expecting the playful, fuzzy collie to bound in from out of the cold. She did not. Nor did she respond to his hushed but harried calls. Moments later, Fred entered his son's room and broke the gut-wrenching news to him with those two words: "Reveille's gone."

Lively, the sophomore Mascot Corporal of Company E-2, burst from his bedroom and rushed into the backyard. He found nothing. He then dashed into the alley behind his parents' home, hoping still that little Rev may have slipped under the fence and was simply exploring new surroundings. But after thirty to forty minutes of frantic, heart-in-his-throat searching throughout the neighborhood, Lively's fears were confirmed. Reveille, the prominent symbol of the proud university, was gone, stolen in the cover of pre-dawn darkness from the Livelys' backyard. The range of sudden emotions spiraling through his body was practically dizzying. Fear, fury, shock, uncertainty, regret, and embarrassment stirred in his stomach in a sickening mixture of mayhem. "I went through so many emotions that it's difficult to recall them all," said Lively, now a captain in the Marine Corps and executive officer for First FAST (Fleet Anti-terrorism Security Team)

Company. "I guess the worst initial feelings were just the helplessness of the situation and then the fear for her safety. Somehow, some way, I desperately wanted to do anything possible to get her back in one, healthy piece."

That would eventually happen, but what transpired over the ensuing six days would add to the legacy of Reveille, thrusting her into the regional spotlight and earning national media attention from New York to Los Angeles. The university's eventual plea of, "bring us back our lost little puppy," struck a chord not just with Aggies, but also with dog owners and animal lovers throughout the state, region, and beyond. In an ironic twist, the end of a boastful claim to fame among many A&M cadets produced an outpouring of sympathy toward the school—even from people who typically disliked or disdained the Aggies. When news of the theft broke and Dallas radio station KYNG-FM offered a one-thousand-dollar reward for Reveille VI's safe return, the station was flooded with calls from concerned A&M fans, along with numerous well-wishers from the University of Texas, Baylor, and various other schools. The fax machines continuously buzzed at newspapers, radio stations, and television studios throughout the state.

The outpouring of love and compassion was even stronger than the frustration among Company E-2 members at the first-ever pilfering of the A&M mascot. In practically every article that had ever been written about the Reveille tradition up to that point, it was noted that she was the only live mascot in the old Southwest Conference never to have been stolen. Essentially, that claim had become the rallying cry of Company

Greg Reils (left) *and Jeff Heath do a little bonding with Reveille VI shortly after her arrival in College Station.*
Courtesy Lee Phillips

TOP DOG

Company E2 cadets (from left) Chris Schuemack, Jeff Lamigo and Spencer Stricklin adopt the Aggie cheer stance at a women's volleyball game.

Cpl. Jim Lively is mascot corporal, a task that lasts a year and involves keeping almost constant company — even in bed.

She's more than a mascot; she's an Aggie. But you can call her 'Miss Reveille, ma'am.'

By Nancy Kruh
Staff Writer of The Dallas Morning News

COLLEGE STATION, Texas — Saying Reveille, the collie mascot at Texas A&M, is just a dog is like saying . . . well, it's like saying the annual A&M-University of Texas matchup is just a football game.

Pardon. Make that texas university (lowercase, please) because, of course, in this part of the state A&M is The University. Just like, in this part of the state, Reveille is not a dog. She is The Dog.

Can't miss her. She's the Lassie look-alike allowed in any A&M building — cafeterias and dorms included. She's the only one who wears the exalted five diamonds, outranking even the commander of the entire 1,900-member A&M Corps of Cadets. And she's the only one with an entire 75-man cadet company — a kind of Aggie Secret Service — dedicated to her round-the-clock care and protection.

Which obviously is why "she's the only mascot in the history of the Southwest Conference never to be stolen," says Jim Lively, the 19-year-old cadet from Dallas who can usually be found at the other end of Reveille's leash. "We take great pride in that. That's something we don't take lightly. Just like you don't joke about bombs at an airport, that (stealing Reveille) is something you don't joke about around here. That's
Please see REVEILLE on Page 4F.

Above: Reveille accompanies the cadets of Company E2 on their afternoon run. Left: The mascot waits patiently for Cpl. Lively.

Photography by Karen Stallwood

The article that inspired University of Texas students to nab Reveille VI appeared in the Dallas Morning News *and quoted Jim Lively as saying that he might need a witness protection program if the mascot was ever stolen under his watch.* Courtesy *Dallas Morning News*

E-2, dating back to the 1950s when Reveille II first moved into the outfit's dorm. Just two months prior to the theft, Lively was asked by the *Dallas Morning News* what would happen if she was stolen under his watch. He replied: "I'd probably end up in something like a witness protection program. I really don't like to think about that."

Now, however, he was not only forced to think about it, but also to agonize about every detail of it. In hindsight, the scenarios and potentially missed clues raced through his mind as quickly as shuffling cards in the hands of a Las Vegas dealer. The unfamiliar vehicles that he occasionally witnessed parked in the alley near his parents' home could have been stalkers waiting for a chance to grab the puppy. Did he remember any faces? Recall any license plates? Could he have possibly anticipated this happening?

Regardless, Lively didn't have time to beat himself up. He tried to remain positive, but he realized that the killing, branding, and maiming of mascots wasn't unprecedented. Following a Texas A&M victory over the University of Texas in 1915, A&M students branded the final score of the game, 13-0, onto the side of UT's steer mascot two years later. Making the best of the situation, Texas students transformed the 13-0 brand into "Bevo," the name for each of the Longhorns' mascots since that time. Of a more serious nature, UT students abducted one of Baylor's cub mascots in 1961, and when the bear turned on the students, they beat it to death with a pipe. North Carolina's live ram mascot, Ramses, also was once found butchered at his home farm, the apparent victim of a so-called prank.

As Lively envisioned little Reveille as a hostage, he could only hope the culprit had a compassionate heart. As he gazed toward the golden fuzz Reveille left behind on his family's living room floor, Lively began to quash his fears by pouring his heart into a plan of action.

Not initially knowing exactly where to turn, Lively placed a call to Greg Riels, the E-2 Company Commander at the time and the Mascot Corporal two years earlier. Conveniently, Jeff Heath, the Mascot Corporal the year before Lively, was spending some time at Riels's home in Kingwood, so the one current and two former handlers put their heads together over the phone lines and came up with a rather off-the-wall story that would add further intrigue to the puppy-napping case. In an effort to keep the incident out of the press for the time being, Riels and Heath advised Lively to tell any media outlets that inquired about the matter that the culprits had taken the wrong dog. Reveille VI's littermate and fellow female, "Aggie," was owned by the Heath family, resided in their home near Austin, and could be produced at any moment deemed necessary.

The hastily hatched plan was to tell the media that Company E-2 had anticipated a dog-napping and that Lively replaced Reveille with her sister, foiling the attempted larceny and leaving the thieves with a cute but unauthentic imitation of the real Rev. At one point during the frantic week, Heath even produced Aggie in Dallas, dressing her in Rev's blanket and parading her in front of his unknowing friends to see if they would notice it was a different dog. Aggie pulled it off without being detected, so it was decided to move forward with the strategy. The ultimate hope of "Operation Con the

The Texas A&M yell leaders and their new yelp leader, Reveille VI, pose in front of the famous 12th Man statue in front of Kyle Field in 1993. Courtesy 12th Man Foundation

Collie-nappers" was that the culprits would release the real Reveille after believing they had nabbed the wrong pup. Even as far-fetched as it may have seemed, that plan almost worked.

The *Dallas Morning News* called the Lively home on the afternoon of December 26, following up on an anonymous phone call the newspaper received from a person claiming to be a University of Texas student and a member of a group named the "Rustlers." The caller claimed responsibility for the heist, saying he and about thirty other UT students had been randomly taking turns stalking the Livelys' home for two months—ever since reading boasts by Corporal Lively in the *Dallas Morning News* that the mascot had never been stolen. The caller informed the newspaper that one person stole the puppy from the Livelys' backyard, adding that "it was easier than hell." When the Livelys told the newspaper that the culprits took the wrong dog, the paper's editors, lacking a police report or other evidence, decided not to pursue the story.

In the meantime, Riels and Heath began crossing the state in a frantic search for the missing canine. The two former Mascot Corporals drove from Kingwood to College Station, picking up E-2 academic advisor Wynn Rosser and military advisor Chief Matthew Brendal along the way to Dallas. Upon their arrival in Dallas, the rescue team went to work. "Except for the guys who took her, no one else knew about it, and we were just trying to get an idea from Jim who might have taken her," Heath recalled. "We're following these kids around, following other people around trying to get an idea of what's going on. We're looking through cracks in backyard fences, looking through peoples' trash, and

Reveille often accompanies her E-2 members on morning runs. Courtesy Kevin Graham

doing whatever else we can think of. But we didn't make any real progress."

After keeping things under wraps for three days and turning up no new leads, Riels and Heath decided to return to College Station to explain the situation to J. Malon Southerland, then the interim vice president for student services at Texas A&M. Riels and Heath arrived on Southerland's doorstep at 9:00 A.M. on December 29 and joined him for a spill-the-beans-and-bacon breakfast at the International House of Pancakes, explaining the situation to Southerland and informing him of their initial statements to the newspaper. Southerland told the two former Mascot Corporals that he would tentatively go along with their story, as long

Reveille VI enjoys the fire at Mascot Corporal Bo Wilson's house on Christmas Day 2000. Rev goes home with her handler during the summers and holidays. Courtesy Bo Wilson

as no one asked him directly about the situation. But if asked at a press conference he was scheduled to attend later that day in conjunction with the Aggies' January 1 Cotton Bowl appearance against Notre Dame, Southerland said he would tell the truth.

"We said, 'Fair enough,'" Heath recalled. "We left Dr. Southerland and went back to Kingwood together. Then I drove from Kingwood to my parents' home in Buda, which is just outside of Austin. Not ten minutes after I walked into the door of my parents' house, the

Austin American Statesman [which had also been contacted by the anonymous member of the Rustlers] called. My dad talked to the reporter, and he said the guys that have Rev VI told [the reporter] that if they see another collie puppy on the Cotton Bowl sidelines, then they'll return this dog to us. So I get on the phone and talked to Greg and Jim and we think, 'Oh, we've got this in the clear. This will work.'"

But things did not go exactly as the cadets planned from that point forward. In what ultimately proved to

be a prudent decision, A&M officials, including Southerland, Rosser, and executive director of university relations Rene Henry, called a press conference in Dallas for Thursday, December 30, to go public with the true story. In a carefully crafted message delivered primarily by Henry, the university pleaded not simply for the return of their mascot, the dog, or even Reveille but, rather, their lost little puppy. The A&M spokesmen also provided an easy way out for the Rustlers, announcing that if the puppy was returned unharmed

Reveille VI and Toto get acquainted prior to the on-campus performance of The Wizard of Oz *as part of MSC OPAS.* Courtesy Cushing Library

Not So Color Blind

Canines are color blind. But how about Reveille?

Dating back to the original Rev, who seemed to recognize khaki, the Reveille mascots have occasionally displayed an ability to distinguish Aggie colors from all others. Case in point: the 1999 Alamo Bowl.

With the Aggies in San Antonio preparing to play Penn State, Mascot Corporal Kevin Graham and Reveille VI attended a variety of events associated with the bowl game. During one of the events, legendary Penn State coach Joe Paterno expressed a desire to meet the famous First Lady of Texas A&M.

"We were backstage in this little amphitheatre with the Penn State cheerleaders, our yell leaders, a couple of team captains from each team, and both head coaches," Graham said. "Well, Joe Paterno walks over and says he wants to meet Rev. Here I am a nineteen-year-old, and I am going, 'Oh my God, Joe Paterno is coming over here.' So I introduced myself to him, and he reaches down to pet Rev, and she just starts growling. She barked at him. I don't think she really cared that he was Joe Paterno. She just saw the other team's uniform and was not real happy. I really think she was going to bite Joe Paterno. She never did anything like that. Unless you were a squirrel or a motorcycle, she was an incredibly pleasant dog to be around."

by 5:00 P.M. on New Year's Eve, A&M would take that into consideration in determining whether or not criminal charges would be filed. The sympathetic tone had its desired effect.

Once the news went public, it made front-page headlines throughout Texas and was even included in news item briefs in the *Los Angeles Times, New York Times, Chicago Tribune,* and other major newspapers across the country. While some readers and listeners laughed it off as a collegiate prank, Aggies, dog lovers, animal rights activists, and even some University of Texas alumni were howling mad about the theft of a puppy. Austin native Irene Knolle, for example, called the *Austin American-Statesman* and said, "I'm a UT grad, and I love dogs. I think this is asinine. The Neanderthals that did this should be expelled." University of Texas president Robert Berdahl was similarly stern in his comments, saying, "This entire incident is a stupid, puerile act. If it was perpetrated by UT students, as alleged, it has achieved nothing except to embarrass UT."

It enraged many Aggies and propelled others into action. At the time, Drew Lanningham, Mascot Corporal for Reveille IV in 1981–82, was a special agent for the U.S. Naval Criminal Investigative Service, a division of the Department of Defense. When he heard of Reveille's abduction, Lanningham was working on an undercover wire tap case with the FBI involving contract fraud and public corruption. With his Aggie blood boiling and his passion for Reveille rising, Lanningham vowed to do something to help. "I basically got law enforcement in the state of Texas to agree that Reveille was state property," Lanningham recalled. "I had to

During televised games, Reveille receives plenty of camera time. But as this FOX Sports Net reporter learns, interviewing Rev could be kind of "ruff." Courtesy Jeff Bailey

make sure I didn't overstep my boundaries because I was a federal agent and this was a state matter. But through some discreet inquiries, I got the Texas Rangers and DPS on the case, and an all points bulletin was issued for Reveille."

Meanwhile, back in Austin, one of the Rustlers, who identified himself as "Bob," met with a reporter from the *Austin American-Statesman*. Bob brought a playful, seemingly healthy Reveille to the meeting with the reporter and said she would not be harmed. He also detailed the Rustlers' ransom demands, which included A&M quarterback Corey Pullig flashing the hook 'em horns hand signal during the Cotton Bowl and A&M officials saying "that UT is better than them." Henry deemed the demands as ludicrous and said the theft should be considered a felony. The puppy would need to be worth at least $750 for third-degree felony charges to be filed, and when Henry was asked about her value, he said she could be worth as much as $1 million to the university in her marketing role and overall importance to the student body. Fred Lively also mentioned the possibility of filing criminal charges. In the aftermath of the theft, he found a door to his home ajar, leading to a suspicion that the Rustlers not only stalked his home for two months and broke into his backyard but also broke into his house. Southerland put down a gauntlet of sorts, as well, telling the *Bryan–College Station Eagle*, "The reality is, as time goes by, it takes more the form of a felony than a prank. Should there be harm to the puppy, we're talking about a most serious situation."

Fortunately, the situation never turned more serious. On New Year's Eve morning, the puppy-nappers con-tacted reporters from the *Austin American-Statesman* and radio station KLBJ, saying Reveille was tied to a "No Trespassing" sign near Lime Creek Road at Lake Travis. Reveille VI was found by Bettye and Bill Langham, who were driving on F.M. 2222 when they heard a radio broadcast about 11:30 A.M. detailing her alleged location. After a little searching, the couple found Reveille, called the Travis County sheriff's department on a mobile phone, and turned her over to two sheriff's deputies who arrived on the scene.

"The sheriff's department called us after picking her up," said Heath, who was back in Dallas by this time. "He said, 'We need somebody who can positively identify this dog. We don't know if this is actually Rev VI. We just know it's a collie.' Well, the only people in Austin who had been around her who could honestly say whether it was or it wasn't her were my parents [Robert and Mary Heath]. So I called them and sent them to the substation to pick her up. Once they reached the substation, they were interviewed and filmed by media outlets all over the state. They knew it was Rev because of some particular markings that she had. After picking her up, they drove her to College Station to see [veterinarian] Dr. Charles Hall. My mom called Dr. Hall's office to tell him they were about ten minutes away, and he said, 'Great, don't step on all the media when you get here.'"

The print reporters and camera crews were swarming the Small Animal Clinic like a stirred ant bed when Reveille arrived. After a fifteen-minute examination, Dr. Hall noted she had a few fleas and seemed a bit thin after her six-day ordeal, but he also said she did not appear to have been mistreated and pronounced her

Neither rain nor sleet nor snow at the Independence Bowl kept Reveille from representing the Aggies on the sidelines. Reveille VI and Mascot Corporal Bo Wilson (with leash) pose for a picture at the frigid 2000 Independence Bowl in Shreveport, La.
Courtesy Bo Wilson

Star attractions meet in Big D, as former Dallas Cowboys quarterback Troy Aikman poses with Reveille VI prior to the Aggies' Cotton Bowl game against UCLA on New Year's Day in 1998. Courtesy Jeff Bailey

fit and ready for Cotton Bowl duty the next afternoon. Reveille received a bath and a dip and spent New Year's Eve at the Small Animal Clinic under Texas A&M University Police protection. At 5:00 A.M. on New Year's Day, Jim Lively and Jeff Heath picked up the pup and drove her back to Dallas for the Aggies' afternoon kickoff against Notre Dame in the 1994 Cotton Bowl, and the headlines in that morning's *Bryan–College Station Eagle* read, "Puppy hostage freed with fleas." When Reveilles V and VI entered the field minutes before the kickoff, the collies received thunderous applause from the crowd. Finally, the ordeal was over, but the aftereffects would continue to produce intriguing and somewhat surprising results.

The Rustlers may have said they stole Reveille to prove a point or to put Aggies in their place by teaching Texas A&M a lesson about making boastful claims. But in wake of the media flurry regarding her theft and return, something of a Reveille renaissance began on the A&M campus and spilled into virtually every nook and cranny of alumni pockets throughout the state. In essence, the theft transformed Rev from a lovable, well-known figure on campus into an Aggieland icon.

Coincidentally, Amy Jaska, a twenty-five-year-old mother from Cedar Park, Texas, began marketing and selling her stuffed Reveille dolls at the Texas A&M bookstore toward the end of the 1993 football season. The timing couldn't have been any better, as adoring fans snatched the dolls from the shelves for their children to cuddle with at bedtime. According to a 1994 story in the *Bryan–College Station Eagle,* Jaska sold twelve hundred of the stuffed pups at thirty dollars apiece in her first year. And that was just the tip of the iceberg in terms of sales. Even today, Holley Scott, the general manager of the Memorial Student Center bookstore on campus, says the dolls are among the best-selling items in the store. "And if they are not buying a doll for their kids, they're usually buying a T-shirt with Reveille on it," Scott said. "Basically, anything that has Reveille on it or serves as a Reveille replica sells extremely well." Nowadays, practically anything could feature Reveille's likeness, including prints, paintings, Christmas cards, coin banks, figurines, dancing dolls,

and even a fifty-minute video tape—*Reveille: My Life as the Aggie Mascot*—starring Reveille V as herself.

The media frenzy regarding Rev also created a dramatic surge in appearance requests for her. During the 1960s, '70s, and even into the '80s, Reveille was seen by the public primarily on campus or at A&M athletic events. As her popularity soared, though, so did the requests for her to appear at fundraisers and regularly scheduled meetings outside the campus setting. According to the Association of Former Students, there are 191 A&M Clubs throughout the state of Texas. At one point or another during the decade of the 1990s and into the twenty-first century, most of those clubs—if not all—requested visits from the First Lady of Aggieland. Viewing it as an opportunity to promote the tradition, Mascot Corporals and Company E-2 members rarely rejected any offer to proudly parade Reveille before the masses. She also has been a regular at Aggie Moms' Club meetings, as well as at numerous other A&M-related mixers, parties, and gatherings.

Even on campus, where students were already accustomed to seeing her, she has become an even more popular attraction in recent years. "I'd have to leave sometimes an hour or hour and a half in advance to get to my class on time just because so many people would stop me with Rev and want to play with her or pet her," said Jordan Caddick, the Mascot Corporal for Reveille VII in 2002–2003. "I'd shine and press my uniform the night before so all I had to do was put it on and go. Most of the time I'd still be late to class with Rev. When you think back fifteen years, there's just no comparison in her popularity from then to now. Her popularity just keeps rising."

No comment, sir. Reveille V seems content as she deals with a reporter after she was jailed on campus as part of an A&M fundraiser. Courtesy Cushing Library

Pictures with Reveille are another activity that supports that assertion. The official, two-day photo session, which doubles as a fundraiser for Reveille's expenses, draws thousands of people, with lines winding through the Memorial Student Center in anticipation of a perfect picture with the beloved mascot. Unofficial photo opportunities are equally popular. Before the start of the 2003 football season, for example, the A&M athletic department held its picture and poster day at Kyle Field, attracting roughly seven to ten thousand camera-toting, autograph-seeking fans in search of players and coaches. The line to meet new A&M head coach Dennis Franchione began to form even before Fran sat down, and it stretched from midfield to beyond the south end zone. But as Reveille arrived and strolled across the field to her position, fans flocked from all other lines for a snapshot with Rev. At its peak, the Reveille line probably surpassed the length of all others, with the possible exception of Franchione's.

The continuation of her escalating fame certainly cannot be attributed solely to the 1993 theft and the media circus that followed, but it is apparent that the incident was a major factor. The mere thought of losing her caused many Aggies to embrace her even more. "I think it's really interesting when you consider that one of the most trying times in Reveille's history has actually spurred her popularity," said Greg Riels. "She led every news story in the state of Texas for two days, and while some people were poking fun of A&M at that time, she was front-page news. If people didn't know about her before that incident, they did following it. I think that's kind of an ironic twist of fate."

Reveille VII poses with some of the memorabilia and collectibles that she inspired in the MSC Bookstore. The stuffed Reveille dolls were introduced in the early 1990s and are a must-have for Aggie children. Courtesy Trey Wright

Another ironic twist involved the fate of the Rustler who eventually claimed responsibility for stealing Reveille from the Livelys' backyard. By early January of 1994, A&M officials and the Lively family decided not to pursue criminal charges against the canine-nappers, choosing instead to leave any disciplinary action to the University of Texas. In fact, the harshest words uttered by A&M officials in the aftermath of the incident were probably directed toward Aggies. "We

[A&M] will prosecute to the fullest anyone who dares try to retaliate," Henry told various media outlets. The warning was apparently heeded, and by February of 1995, the indignation had begun to fade, at least until a story in the University of Texas' student newspaper revived the issue. According to the story in the *Daily Texan,* UT student Neil Sheffield admitted to stealing the mascot and was using the information as a publicity stunt to help him win an election for Student Association president. In a campaign flier for Sheffield's ticket, he listed the top ten reasons he should be elected. Number four on the list read, "Neil Sheffield stole Reveille, the Aggies' mascot. Pretty darn cool, huh?"

Aggies weren't the only ones who didn't find humor in the stunt or the admission that Sheffield was the thief in Lively's backyard. The Election Supervi-

sory Board disqualified Sheffield from the race after he was quoted in the *Daily Texan* saying, "A year and a half ago, I knew completely that I was doing it for the sole purpose of running for president." Sheffield appealed, but the UT Judicial Commission upheld the decision to disqualify him. Sheffield responded to the verdict by calling the Election Supervisory

Whether by train, plane, or automobile, Reveille has become quite the traveler. Rev VII loads up for another tour of Texas. During the summer of 2003, she was also spotted in a ski lift at the 12th Man Foundation summer board meeting in Keystone, Colorado. Courtesy Jerred Crumley

Board "a bunch of Aggies." But in this particular case, it was probably the Aggies who had reason to smile. While Sheffield was disqualified from his election, Lively would eventually be elected as a class agent at Texas A&M.

Lively rebounded from the entire incident like an NBA power forward. He was immediately absolved by fellow members of Company E-2, who were outspoken in their support and in their defense of Lively's reputation. Following the 1994 Cotton Bowl, however, Lively initially loathed the mere thought of going back to classes when the spring semester started in mid-January. Reveille VI was healthy, famous, and back at the end of Lively's leash, but going back to classes meant feeling the stares of students who had followed the theft from start to finish. How would the general

Two Texas traditions—Reveille and bluebonnets. Courtesy Jeff Bailey

student body react to him? Would he hear their whispers or see their rolling eyes? Lively faced a number of fears when he first determined that Reveille was gone. Now, it was time to do it again.

"It was almost a full month from when she was stolen to when classes started," Lively recalled. "When I was walking to class and people were doing double-takes and asking questions, it was difficult simply because Reveille had never been stolen. So, it was just a matter of me looking people in the eyes like, 'Yeah, I was the one. That was me.' That's just the reality of life. But as a twenty-year-old, that certainly built a lot of character. After going through that trying time, I feel like I can handle about anything. I was never blacklisted or mistreated at A&M, and I had the full support of great guys like Greg Riels and Jeff Heath. But it was a character test for me, and the overall level of support and encouragement I received is a testament to the outfit, the Corps of Cadets, and the type of people A&M produces. But what else would you expect from a university that even treats its mascot like part of the family?"

While Lively may ultimately have been better off for persevering through the character tests of the theft, the incident proved to be only the beginning of difficult times for Reveille VI. The cute little puppy, whose picture was once plastered on the front pages of newspapers across the state, matured into a vibrant, beautiful collie. Her six days as a hostage did nothing to dampen her spirit, her temperament, or her warm personality. She loved her Frisbee, adored her cadets, preferred to sleep in the closet or any other burrowlike setting, and possessed an amazing memory regarding everyone who had played a significant role in her life.

Reveille VI and Mascot Corporal Jeff Bailey receive the red carpet treatment at a function in Houston sponsored by Purina. Several Houston-area celebrities were invited to attend the event with their dogs. Rev was certainly the best-behaved, especially compared to some ill-mannered rottweilers, who attempted to attack several other dogs and dog owners. Courtesy Jeff Bailey

During the summer of 2003, Reveille VI enjoyed a boat ride with her retirement caretaker, Dr. Charles Hall.
Courtesy Dr. Charles Hall

"Rev VI had a really sweet disposition, and she was very smart," said Craig Serold, the Mascot Corporal in 1998–99. "She was so intelligent that she knew she could get away with things that no other person— let alone another dog—could do. She just had this air, or confidence, about her. She knew she was the center of attention everywhere she went, and she enjoyed that, for the most part. But she also knew when she could let her hair down, so to speak, and play like a dog. She definitely knew exactly what she liked and what she didn't like, and she wasn't shy about letting you know about it."

Among the things she disliked the most were other animals. While she had a certain amount of respect for other dogs she encountered, Rev VI despised squirrels and took much delight in chasing them up trees on campus. But she didn't only pick on animals smaller than her or even those her own size. Perhaps because of her ego, which grew over time as she began to sense her importance on campus, Reveille VI assumed she could take on any four-legged counterpart. That was especially true on game days. Reveille VI enjoyed barking at Bevo nearly as much as she did tormenting squirrels. On a 1997 trip to Boulder, Colorado, Mascot Corporal Jeff Bailey wrestled with Reveille to prevent her from running after Ralphie, the University of Colorado's 1,300-pound buffalo mascot. "She had such a playful side, and at my house she'd do routes around the living room and cut the carpet up while pretending to chase something," Bailey said. "But she also had a serious chasing mode. She really wanted a piece of Ralphie. I don't know what she would have done if I had allowed her to go after Ralphie, but she was pretty fearless."

Or so it seemed. While crowd noise and monstrous mascots rarely fazed her, particularly piercing or unfamiliar noises terrified Reveille VI, triggering epileptic seizures that plagued her throughout her duties as mascot. She suffered her first seizure after the 1995 Alamo Bowl. Following the Aggies' upset victory over Michigan, thousands of multicolored balloons were released from the rafters of San Antonio's Alamodome. Celebrating Texas A&M players and fans stomped on the balloons once they reached the ground, producing intense popping sounds that triggered the seizure. According to medical records, she endured at least five seizures from December 29, 1995, to September 17,

1996. She also suffered a grand mal seizure and was presented to the Animal Emergency Clinic in St. Louis following the Aggies' Big 12 championship game victory over Kansas State on December 5, 1998.

Veterinarians combated the condition with Phenobarbital, which reduced the occurrences of the seizures and prolonged her ability to serve as the mascot, but the constant medications took their toll on Reveille VI. A sedative, Phenobarbital controlled the epileptic attacks, but it is toxic to the liver, and the continued doses all but destroyed the organ by the time she was officially retired as mascot in the spring of 2001. Under normal circumstances, her funeral probably would have occurred within the same calendar year as her retirement. But Texas A&M is not a normal veterinary school, Reveille is not a normal dog, and Rev's foster parents, Dr. Charles Hall and his wife, Diana, are certainly not the typical pet owners. Dr. Hall, who came to A&M as a student in 1951 and joined the faculty of the veterinary school in 1967, first volunteered to be the primary care provider for Reveille IV. He also served as Reveille V's and VI's veterinarian until his retirement in 1995.

When Reveille VI retired into his home in 2001, Hall said, she was practically a zombie. He decided to start backing her off the Phenobarbital immediately, and over the next two months, her activity and alertness increased dramatically. But soon after taking a turn for the better, she began losing her appetite, dropping weight and barely resembling the vibrant mascot that once was willing to battle a buffalo. "We had her evaluated, and they told us there was no way she could survive much longer," Dr. Hall recalled. "They went into

Well-wishers gathered on the Zone Plaza at Kyle Field on November 2, 2003, to pay their final tributes to Reveille VI.
Courtesy Trey Wright

the abdomen with an arthroscopic camera and took pictures of her liver, and it looked horrible. The numbers on her liver function test were terrible, too. They just said she couldn't live. But we had them put in an indwelling tube through her neck, into her esophagus, and down into her stomach. We started feeding her a special diet and giving her medication over the next

five months. She continued to decline for quite some time and went down from her normal weight of fifty-seven or fifty-eight pounds to forty-four pounds."

At her worst, Reveille VI resembled a fur-covered skeleton, but instead of wilting away, she bounced back with an amazing resiliency. Even when she began accumulating more than two gallons of fluid in her abdomen and looked as if she was pregnant, Reveille VI didn't give up the fight. Her failing liver couldn't deal with the fluids, but she had the heart to hold on. Over the next several months, she improved so much that Hall finally decided to remove the tube and allow her to eat on her own. "It's been a long recovery, but she has lost all of the fluid in her abdomen, added ten pounds—from forty-four to fifty-four—and is doing very well," Hall said in the summer of 2003, while on a cross-country road trip with his wife and Reveille. "Her behavior and activity are indicative of a happy dog again. She's chasing the Frisbee again, and she is enjoying the traveling. She's been through a lot, but she's our little warrior."

She stared the grim reaper in the eyes as an adult and didn't flinch. She also served as a puppy hostage and didn't seem to mind. Reveille VI's life wasn't always easy, but she lived it with a passion to play and an apparent enjoyment of her purpose as mascot. In terms of overall years as the university's mascot (seven and a half), she served a shorter time than any of her predecessors, but on a regional and even national level, she may have made the biggest impact of all the Reveilles. She survived the Rustlers, the seizures, and even liver failures before the decision was made that her time had come and she was euthanized on October 18, 2003. And while she may not have enjoyed tremendous longevity on campus, she certainly left a lasting legacy.

With all of her duties and her dignitary-like status on campus, Reveille truly seems to enjoy letting her hair down, so to speak, and just being a dog. Rev VI joins Mascot Corporal Kevin Graham in the lake. Courtesy Kevin Graham

CHAPTER 5

Retirement Home

EVOLUTION OF A TRADITION

IT DOESN'T USUALLY happen anymore. Time, for the most part, has eased those sorrows and made it possible to recall and recite all the memories with dry eyes. But even now, there are unpredictably rare moments when the clean, fur-free carpets and tidy stacks of folded towels produce reminders of the way things used to be when Reveille IV made their house her home. And as strange as it may seem to some, especially non-pet owners, Lee and Joanne Phillips miss the mounds of shedding, sable hair and the strewn pieces of torn towels. Most of all, they miss the magic and warmth Rev IV brought to their home and the smiles she continually placed on their own faces for nearly five years.

She was never really their personal pet. Although she lived with them, the Phillipses always believed—and always informed others—that Reveille still belonged to Texas A&M, Company E-2, and the university's stu-dent body. The Phillipses primarily viewed the retired mascot as a distinguished guest on an extended stay. Reveille, on the other hand, made it clear she felt completely at home in the Phillipses' house in Bryan, Texas. From the day she arrived on December 4, 1984, until her death on March 29, 1989, Rev IV filled the Phillipses' home with more life and more memories than they ever could have possibly imagined.

She loved her "canine quarters," which members of Company E-2 constructed when the Phillipses were chosen as her retirement care providers. The ten-by-seventeen-foot room in the back of the Phillipses' home—an area that was once their back patio—featured carpet, air conditioning, a ceiling fan, numerous pictures of Rev, a "doggy door," and even a cable outlet in case she wanted to watch her Aggies on TV. Rev's old room is now a virtual shrine to the tradition of Reveille and the Mascot Corporals through the years. In her retirement, Reveille IV loved to play, chasing her Frisbee relentlessly across the yard and engaging Lee Phillips in feisty tug-of-war battles with the towels used to dry her off. She would dig her feet into the living room carpet and tug until the towel was little more than cloth confetti. She also seemed to embrace her new role as a family pet. Although the Phillipses never considered themselves her owner, she adopted them. One of the highlights of Lee Phillips's typical work day unfolded when he turned onto his cul-de-sac and caught his first glimpse of Reveille basking in the sunlight on the small hill in his front yard.

Shortly before Phillips would return home from campus, where he was an industrial engineering professor, Joanne would allow Reveille to enter the front yard. Rev would position herself in a pose atop the slope and wait patiently for Phillips's red pickup truck to turn the corner. Once the truck came into her view, she would rise, wait until he pulled into the driveway, and follow the truck back to the garage, taking delight in being first to greet Phillips at the end of another work day. "She was just so beautiful sitting out in the front yard, as if she was posing for a picture," Phillips said nostalgically. "She had so much grace, and we were so proud to have her in our home. One of the secretaries I worked with made a sign for my truck that said, 'Reveille IV on board.' She'd sit in the passenger seat, and I'd put that sign in the window as we drove around town. I don't know who was prouder—her or me—when we were running errands. We didn't know what we were getting ourselves into when we accepted her into our home, but it was really such a

Former Mascot Corporal Jeff Gruetzmacker (left) *originally chose Company E-2 because it was a Navy–Marine Corps outfit. He initially knew nothing about the Reveille tradition. But when the lifelong dog owner learned of Rev and met then–commanding officer Kevin Bark, he figured E-2 was the perfect fit.* Courtesy Jeff Gruetzmacker

*Reveille VI receives an approving glance from former president of the United States
George H. W. Bush as Mascot Corporal Mark Boynton looks on.* Courtesy Joe West

wonderful experience for us. I really believe the retirement was good for her, and I know for a fact that it was a blessing for us."

The retirements of Reveille have been one of the most beneficial additions—for both the canine and her human home owners—in the evolution of the tradition. Reveille IV was the first A&M mascot to be retired from the public spotlight into a private home, and her experience was so positive that retirement has become an accepted, recommended, and cherished component of the tradition. For Company E-2 and the student body at large, retiring Reveille has provided an opportunity to close a chapter in the tradition without closing a casket at the same time. For the chosen Aggie families who have accepted Reveilles into their homes, the experience has been both humbling and heartwarming. And for the actual mascots, the benefits of retirement are almost too numerous to list. First and foremost, though, retirement has added years to their existence and magnified their quality of life.

While Reveille may be one of the most beloved, cherished, and adored canines in the country, she is also under more stress and consistently subject to far more demands than most other four-legged counterparts. Lassie, Benji, and other Hollywood canine stars rarely went to work without stand-ins, doubles, and even triples, but Reveille is expected to be on the job and on her best behavior without any relief in sight. While she is not often required to jump through hoops or perform a vast array of tricks on command, she is under constant scrutiny. She may engage more people on a typical football game weekend than a campaigning politician, while posing for more pictures than a

swimsuit model on a photo shoot. The constant travels, the annual changing of handlers, the daily runs with Company E-2, the marches, life in the dorm, the decibel levels of a sold-out Kyle Field, the heat and humidity of College Station, and the never-ending public appearances before her fans of all ages can take a toll on Reveille over time.

Especially when age-related limitations and medical conditions such as arthritis begin to set in, retiring Reveille is a humane, life-prolonging decision. Reveille IV was retired before her tenth birthday, as was Reveille V. In their retirement settings, both former mascots greatly exceeded the average life expectancy of American collies, which, according to various sources, is ten to twelve years. Both Reveille IV and V lived until they were almost fifteen, the human equivalent of over one hundred years old. Primarily because of her epilepsy and other related ailments, Reveille VI was retired before her eighth birthday. Considering the number of life-threatening battles she waged early in retirement, Reveille VI also surpassed all veterinary estimates for her life expectancy, surviving more than a month past her tenth birthday. She probably would have died much sooner if not for being placed into the home of Dr. Charles and Diana Hall, two animal lovers with decades of veterinary experience and a particular passion for the Reveille tradition.

When Dr. Hall was initially contacted about accepting the retired Reveille into his home, he agreed primarily because he considered his wife, a former veterinary technician, to be the best animal caretaker in the world. The Halls already owned three dogs and two cats and several other animals, but Dr. Hall knew

Reveille is no prima donna, but nobody can begrudge the First Lady of Aggieland a chance to admire herself in a dorm-room mirror. Courtesy Cushing Library

that Reveille was his wife's favorite Aggie tradition. Her reaction to his proposal of taking Reveille into their home was even better than he anticipated. "I asked her if she would consider adopting Reveille in retirement, and we ended up doing a dance afterward," Dr. Hall said. "She was thrilled. You couldn't give Reveille to any person who would have been happier than Diana was at the thought of Reveille becoming her adopted child."

While Company E-2 has made a number of outstanding decisions regarding the Reveille tradition, among the finest have been the selections of the Phillipses, Wests, and Halls as Rev's retirement families. They not only cared for Rev in her final days, but also catered to her every need. The animals obviously received the top veterinary care available from Texas A&M's Small Animal Clinic. Many pet owners could not afford or provide the type of preventative and prolonging medical attention the Reveilles received. Without a doubt, retirement has been extremely beneficial for the former mascots. So good, in fact, that there is a considerable movement to retire future Reveilles at an even earlier age—regardless of whether their physical condition mandates it.

"When you really try to view things from the dog's perspective, Reveille gives so much to the university, and I think she deserves to spend the final years of her life in a quiet, normal setting," said Dr. Claudia Barton, the primary veterinarian now in charge of Reveille's care. "She has an awful lot of stresses and demands that are unnatural for a dog. And even the yearly changing of Mascot Corporals deprives her of the typical attachments to one owner that normal dogs would enjoy. What I have seen is that retiring these animals has

Expense Account

While Reveille has always been a popular attraction among traveling A&M fans and even opponents' fans on the road, the expenses for Rev's travels—and those of her handlers—have not always been covered by the university. Up until Drew Lanningham served as Reveille IV's Mascot Corporal in 1981–82, any expenses incurred for travels with Reveille came out of the Mascot Corporal's pocket.

Fortunately for the A&M fans who love to see Rev on the road, and thankfully for the handlers who love to show Reveille off, that changed in 1981–82. "Reveille IV was the first Reveille who had a fund established where the people who donated to it, whether it be private or whatever, funded all of her needs—veterinary needs, her travel, travel for the Mascot Corporal, et cetera," Lanningham said. "What I originally had to do was use my own money, or my dad's credit card, for travel expenses. That fund was started in the middle of my time as the Mascot Corporal, because I vocally spoke out that you had to have Reveille at a game, and students and former students would be shocked if they knew that the outfit and the Mascot Corporal were having to fund the whole thing without any donations or any help from the university. But after that point, donations made that fund possible, and that was very important because it made sure that she was at all major events and that it didn't stress out the sophomore to have to dish out his own money. It also made it more professional, organized, and worthwhile."

Although she may be the most recognized member of the Corps of Cadets, Reveille also has her own student ID card. Rev VI's card shown here was the first one issued. Courtesy Kevin Graham

been very good for the dog, and that's why we've recommended that future mascots be retired after about six to eight years. That may mean that we have three Revs still alive at any given time. That would make them the symbol of the university for a shorter time, and it would allow them to have a normal dog's life for a greater time. Anybody who loves dogs and wants what's best for them would want that for Reveille, I think."

That's not the only change Barton and others associated with the university want to see implemented in the best interest of the mascot. While virtually everyone loves to exalt the arrival of a cute, fuzz-covered puppy, Barton's recommendation is that future Reveilles should not begin their role as the "official" mascot until they are at least one year old and have completed a comprehensive training program. Presenting

Former Mascot Corporal Craig Serold poses with Reveille V (right) *and Rev VI in Joe and Carrie West's backyard. Members of Company E-2 regularly visit the retired Revs.* Courtesy Joe West

a tiny puppy before a huge crowd and holding her up like Simba in *The Lion King* makes for good theater and photo opportunities. But it is probably not in the best interest of the animal. When Reveille VII was selected, a request was made to present her on the A&M campus at just six weeks old. Barton nixed that request, saying it was inappropriate to transport her from her birth place in Florida before she finished her first series of vaccinations. So Reveille VII was allowed to finish her shots, and, since she was the only puppy in her mother's womb, she was placed with a litter of ten other puppies to enhance her socialization skills. As a result,

Reveille VII was presented at a Texas A&M basketball game at four months old, but even that was probably too early, Barton says. Rev was immediately and noticeably "spooked" by the volume of the band, especially the tubas.

Prior to arriving in College Station, Rev VII was exposed to some loud noises, as her breeders, Dr. Cindi Bossart and her husband, James Efron, frequently turned up the volume of their big-screen television set as loud as it would go during sporting events. The couple also played loud music and simulated crowd noise. But it's difficult to imitate the volume of Aggieland

The only Reveille to have puppies was Rev II. But Reveille VI serves as a surrogate mother to the Bailey family pet's pups.
Courtesy Jeff Bailey

Reveille VII with Mascot Corporal Bo Wilson and her stuffed Bevo doll. Notice the "13-0" on Bevo's side, which A&M students branded into the UT mascot two years after the 1915 A&M-UT game. Texas students transformed the brand into "Bevo," the name of each of the Longhorns' mascots since that time. Courtesy Bo Wilson

and, in hindsight, more simulation and training time would have probably been beneficial to Reveille VII before her acclimation to Texas A&M. This will probably be an added element of the training of future Reveilles.

"Once she arrived, I started thinking that putting a four-month-old puppy into a situation where she has all these engagements and can't even take a nap in the afternoon is about like putting a five- or six-year-old child in that setting," Barton said. "In the future, I'd

Young Reveille VII takes a look at her new surroundings in the dorm rooms on the quad at Texas A&M.
Courtesy Bo Wilson

really like to see us pick the Reveille, introduce her, and then send her away to training for a year. Texas A&M is now this giant university, and the alumni kind of feel like they own Reveille, so it's even more important that we have the chance to assess the personality of this dog. Maybe this little puppy that we hold up at the game is going to turn out to have a temperament that is not appropriate, and then we sort of have a chance to say, 'OK, we're going to pick a different one.' A stable, quiet temperament is so essential to a dog that will be going to kindergarten classes, meeting digni-

taries, attending sporting events, and so forth. She has to be a pretty fearless dog, and that first year of training would allow us to expose her to as many stimuli as possible to be sure she can handle it and thrive in the midst of all the attention."

The Reveille tradition began receiving even more attention in the aftermath of the tragic 1999 Aggie Bonfire collapse. While it may seem like a stretch to draw a correlation between the mascot tradition and the fallen logs that killed twelve people and injured many more, the common denominator is potential lawsuits. The collapse of Bonfire resulted in a series of suits filed against the university, and in assessing other potential grievances, A&M officials determined that a proactive risk management plan needed to be created to cover all student activities. Among the various traditions the university addressed, a committee was formed to focus on the practices and typical demands placed upon Reveille. What the committee discovered upon closer examination was a disturbing trend of increasing activity that placed heavy burdens on Reveille and potentially placed the Mascot Corporals in harm's way.

It was certainly not intentional on Company E-2's part. The outfit regularly goes to extraordinary lengths to preserve, protect, and promote the Reveille tradition. The problem, in a nutshell, was that Company E-2 members, and especially the Mascot Corporals, were probably going too far—quite literally, in fact. As Reveille's appearance requests skyrocketed, so did the miles the Mascot Corporals put on their vehicles. Recognizing her valuable role in public relations, Mascot Corporals rarely said "no" to any request for an appearance. The droopy-eyed handlers crisscrossed the state on road trips with Rev, pumping gas into their cars and trucks and caffeine into their veins. Because of the randomness of the requests, it wasn't unusual for the cadets and the canine to be in West Texas on one day, along the Gulf Coast the next, and to be back in West Texas on the following day. It also wasn't uncommon for some of the more recent Mascot Corporals to drive fourteen, fifteen, or even sixteen thousand miles during a summer's worth of appearances with Reveille.

Upon further investigation, university officials discovered that at least one Mascot Corporal had been involved in an auto accident on a particularly long road trip. Ultimately, university officials decided they needed to put into writing specific restrictions and guidelines regarding Reveille's and the Mascot Corporal's travels. The university also needed to encourage handlers to say "no" to some appearance requests, especially those that required abnormal travel conditions or non-university-related events such as weddings and private receptions.

But it wasn't only travel issues that raised eyebrows among university officials. In 1999, Reveille VI bit a young child when his elementary school took a field trip to Kyle Field. Although the child was not seriously injured and no lawsuits were filed, red flags were raised. When the mascot committee was formed in 2002, virtually every possible Reveille activity was addressed, and her overall role as the university mascot was defined. The committee, composed of university officials and students of varying backgrounds, provided a list of detailed recommendations that ultimately became a conclusive document entitled the "Standard Operating Procedures for Reveille." The twenty-four-point document covered these issues: Purpose of Reveille, Football Games, March-ins and Reviews, Midnight Yell Practice at Home Games, Scheduling Reveille Appearances, Transportation Guidelines to Off-Campus Events, Duties of Assistant Mascot Corporal, Away Football Games, University Credit Card, Grooming,

Revving Up with Rev

Over the years, being on the road with Reveille has produced plenty of memorable moments for the Mascot Corporals. And in the course of crisscrossing the Lone Star State with one of the most prominent and recognizable faces in Texas A&M history, there are also plenty of predictable moments

"When I was traveling to all the clubs and meetings in the summer, there were a lot of one-sided conversations with Reveille," said Kevin Graham, the Mascot Corporal in 1999–2000. "But driving on the road with Rev was always funny. You'd pass Old Ags and lean over and wave or give them the Gig 'em sign. They would give me the Gig 'em back and then give me a blank look when they saw Rev's face in the window. It was so funny, because when you would pass them and pull over in front of them, it was like clockwork. You could count to about twenty, and sure enough they would come speeding up next to me, mouthing the words, 'Is that Rev?' I had people driving down the highway taking pictures of Rev. That happened to me quite a bit."

Reveille VII enjoys a little R&R with her Company E-2 mates. Rev has strict guidelines to follow on game days but may attend the Company E-2 picnics after her nap. Courtesy Jordan Caddick

General Care, Healthcare, Public Appearances, Feeding, Training Treats, Guidelines for Picture Taking, Football Game vs. t.u. in Austin, Earning Reveille, Come-bys, Mascot Corporal Selection, Mascot Chain of Command, Mascot Vacation Accommodations, Changes to the SOPs, and Operational Plan for the Passing Away of Reveille.

Within each of the Standard Operating Procedures is a detailed listing of what is expected, permitted, and required. For example, Reveille's SOP regarding football games covers everything from when, where, and how she should enter the field to the proper procedures for exiting the playing surface, including the "block" that Company E-2 freshmen form around her for her protection. That particular SOP also covers a number of interesting items, such as procedures for when the temperature is above 85 degrees and limitations placed on Rev following the game. According to the document, "After game day activities are completed, Reveille will return to her dormitory room and be given uninterrupted rest for at least one hour. [She] will not participate in any other activities which could induce high levels of stress for the rest of the post-game day, and once rested, [she] may be taken to the Company E-2 picnic, where she will rest in the shade and visit with members and families of Company E-2."

While some alumni and Company E-2 members may have viewed the committee, along with its Standard Operating Procedures, as meddling with tradition, university officials contend that the document was designed to ensure the continuation of Reveille on campus. "Reveille is a tradition that has stood the test of time since the 1930s," said Wynn Rosser, the assistant vice president of student affairs and a former academic advisor to Company E-2. "And I think all Aggies want to make sure that she continues to be a symbol of our university. But her role and activities had increased so much over the years that it was necessary to sit down and say, 'Hey, are all these things in the best interest of the dog and the Mascot Corporals?' With the increase in her popularity, Reveille has come under some unrealistic expectations, and we've tried to humanize her. She's not a human; she's a dog, and dogs have their own wants, needs, and desires that we have attempted to assess. When it is 100 degrees on Kyle Field, we've said in the Standard Operating Procedures that she needs to have a mesh coat, not a wool one. We've said

that she needs water bowls and a cool, shady place to take her when it's particularly hot. That means taking her in and out of the stadium, which some people immediately perceive as a change and then conclude the tradition is under siege. But what we have actually done is protect the dog and done what's best for the dog. And in other cases, we have implemented plans to protect the handlers. There is a rationale and a reason for putting these things in writing. It's not just change for the sake of change or clamping down on Company E-2."

According to Col. Anthony W. Groves, the advisor to the Reveille tradition in Texas A&M's Office of the Commandant, the implementation of the procedures has been smooth and has produced positive results. So has the increased emphasis on providing more training earlier in life. Shortly after Reveille VII arrived on campus, Dr. Barton contacted Dr. Kay Stephens, a fellow veterinarian and the owner of Puppy Love Training and Behavior Counseling center in Navasota, about enrolling little Reveille and her Mascot Corporal, Javier Aguirre, in a basic puppy obedience class. "Rev Sev," as she is known to Company E-2 members, may be the most beautiful and brilliant of the A&M mascots. In fact, she sometimes appears more inclined for the SATs than menial commands such as "sit." But her remarkable canine IQ isn't necessarily a good thing when it comes to performing tedious tasks or standing around for hours at a game or a photo session. Like an intellectual child, Reveille VII tends to bore quickly if she is not constantly challenged, engaged, or entertained. Combined with her herding instincts and easily excitable nature, Rev Sev was quite a handful for her early handlers.

Jeff Bailey gives Reveille VI a lift as a young fan meets the First Lady of Texas A&M.
Courtesy Jeff Bailey

She performed well in her puppy obedience class. But during the 2001 football season, she was occasionally out of control, nipping at her handlers, lunging toward the field, barking incessantly, and testing her two-legged partners. By January of 2002, the decision was made to send Reveille VII back to obedience school—this time as a full-time student. She was taken out of the dorm and placed in Dr. Stephens's home for around-the-clock instruction. For Stephens, a former student at Texas A&M, it was both a challenge and a thrill to work full-time with the mascot of her alma mater. For Reveille, it was time to meet her match, as Dr. Stephens's years of canine training experience meant Rev would no longer rule the roost. For Company E-2, relinquishing complete control of Reveille was a sacrifice that eventually paid positive dividends. At the end of seven months in Dr. Stephens's home, Reveille was far more controllable. When she attended the first game of the 2002 football season, in fact, she may have been more docile than her handlers had hoped.

"There are always going to be some issues with her and future collies, which are hard-wired from generations of breeding, that we are not going to change,"

Blind Ambition

Reveille has never actually been to the White House, but she did attend the inauguration of President George W. Bush in 2001. The trip to Washington, D.C., produced plenty of memorable moments for Reveille, her handler, Bo Wilson, and other members of Company E-2.

Among other events, Rev attended the official black-tie inauguration event, visited Congress, and made an appearance at an event of the Washington, D.C., A&M club.

"That weekend was probably the most hectic weekend I had ever been a part of," Wilson said. "Everywhere we went, people thought we were in the Secret Service. We had on our uniforms, and people didn't know who we were. Some people thought Rev was a drug dog. We went down to the subway, and they wouldn't let her on, so I pretended like I was blind. We had cops coming up saying, 'Is there anything we can get you? Is there anything you need?' I'd say, 'No. Thank you, though.' And I'd be staring out. You'd get the funniest reaction from people, because they'd start staring at you, because they didn't think you could see them. When we took her into the actual banquet, people like the lead singers from ZZ Top came over to have their picture taken with her. That was pretty cool. Miss Texas would not leave until she got a picture with Reveille. It's like traveling with a celebrity, and you can get into so many places you otherwise wouldn't even get into. I guarantee you I would never have been at the inauguration without being with Reveille. I was looking out for her, but she's the one that got me in the door."

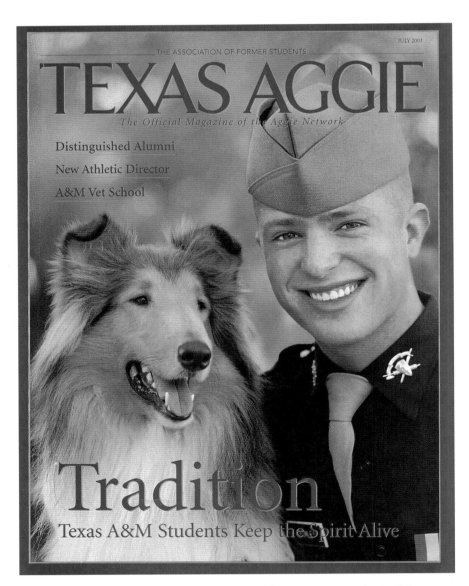

Reveille VII and Jerred Crumley adorn the cover of Texas Aggie *magazine in July, 2003.*
Courtesy the Association of Former Students

Reveille VI, accompanied here by Mascot Corporal Bo Wilson, made the trip to Washington, D.C., for the inauguration of President George W. Bush in 2001. Courtesy Bo Wilson

said Dr. Stephens. "It's kind of like putting a square peg into a round hole in that we often expect her to stand around for hours and look stately and beautiful. That's not her instincts and that's not her temperament, especially during a game when people are screaming and things seem out of control to her. But she's a very bright dog and has made remarkable strides. As long as her handler keeps her occupied—giving her treats, chew toys, commands, and constantly engaging her—she can be very well-behaved. With all the things the handlers do, I think they have the most difficult job on campus, maybe especially with this particular Reveille. She is a sweet, bright dog, but she will test them again and again to see how far she can go. She has a lot of life in her."

It's a life that will be celebrated and documented with virtually every paw print she makes. And it won't stop when her life ends. Perhaps no other university pays such homage to its deceased mascots as Texas A&M. In fact, most universities don't even come close. The original Shasta, the University of Houston's live cougar mascot, was skinned after being donated to the Houston Zoo. According to Bill Little, the highly respected former sports information director at the University of Texas and now a special assistant to the football coach for communications, the original Bevo—the one A&M students branded—was in 1921 the main course at a barbecue hosted by UT officials and attended by Aggie guests. Many other schools either cremate their deceased mascots or bury them unceremoniously in country fields. Not Reveille, though.

All of the Reveilles have received full military honors at their funerals, while flags on campus have flown at half staff. The number of Aggies in attendance at the

Reveille VII, with her "gentle lead" pulled over her snout, participates in march-in with Company E-2. Photo by Allen Pearson, courtesy Texas A&M University Relations

funerals has generally increased with the passing of each mascot. Reveille IV's funeral attendance in 1989—estimated conservatively at more than ten thousand—was even noted on *Ripley's Believe It or Not*. While the original Reveille's coffin was apparently fairly simple, the caskets too have become more elaborate over time. When Reveille V died in 1999, thirty-one members of Company E-2's sophomore class met at a ranch in Clifton, Texas, to begin construction of her coffin. When completed, it was a beautiful, cherry wood casket that included brass handrails and satin lining. As a continuing tribute to the deceased mascots, members of Company E-2 clean the gravesites and place maroon and white flower bouquets on each of the tombstones prior to all home football games. "I know a lot of people outside the A&M family don't understand it, but it really is an honor for us to pay tribute to these mascots who have served our university so well," said Jordan Caddick, the Mascot Corporal in 2002–2003. "When you think about all the things these animals have done to promote the university and to serve the student body, what we do to honor them in death is quite appropriate. And I think it is just another example of the incredibly strong feelings Aggies have for Reveille in life and death."

Many of those Aggies contacted the university to express their strong feelings in 1997 when the proposed renovation of Kyle Field tampered with the burial tradition of Reveille. When the original Reveille died in 1944, she was laid to rest outside the north entrance of the stadium. Reveilles II, III, and IV were also buried in the same location with their faces and paws pointed toward the large opening in the old horseshoe of the

north end zone. According to A&M legend, the Reveilles were buried in that manner so they could always see the scoreboard on the south end of the stadium. But the $32.9 million expansion of the stadium's north end required tearing down the old horseshoe, bulldozing the area outside the stadium, and—to the chagrin of many—relocating the buried Reveilles. As soon as the plan was publicly unveiled, former Texas A&M athletic director Wally Groff was bombarded with e-mails and phone calls from hundreds of outraged fans and alumni. The overwhelming theme of the correspondence was that A&M's athletic department should either scrap the project altogether or build the facility around the Reveille graves.

Groff, who graduated from A&M in 1964 and served within the athletic department for more than thirty-five years, understood the passion Reveille inspired and handled the situation as gently as possible. He personally answered every e-mail and attempted to calm the masses by explaining the long-term plan, which included making the new Reveille gravesites a focal point of the Zone Plaza. Groff's message eased the anger of some fans—at least those who sympathized with the need for Kyle Field's facelift and increased seating capacity. Others, however, were still outraged at the mere thought of exhuming the bones of the beloved mascots. "We worked with Company E-2, Dr. Malon Southerland (the vice president of student affairs), and others," Groff said, "in an effort to move the graves in a professional, tasteful manner. It was simply not feasible to build the new facility without moving the graves. And now, what I really believe you have is a much more attractive tribute to the Reveille tradition."

The First Lady of Texas A&M is front and center in any crowd on campus, even in the company of University President Robert M. Gates. Photo by Allen Pearson, courtesy Texas A&M University Relations

In August of 1997, however, the protests were still being voiced when members of Company E-2 placed green sheets of plastic up around the original, 144-square-foot gravesite to block the view of onlookers. The outfit built new coffins to transfer the remains of the deceased mascots and began the delicate digging process. All four coffins, along with the tombstones, were transferred across Joe Routt Boulevard to a temporary site in Cain Park, where the remains were reburied. In the midst of the digging and transferring, approximately twenty protesters—most members of a group referring to themselves as "Friends of Reveille"—gathered at the site and conducted an impromptu press conference. It produced a few interesting quotes, video clips and sound bites, but it did nothing to deter the move.

By the time the transfer was complete, the temporary gravesite in Cain Park appeared tasteful in the eyes of most A&M supporters and acceptable to many Reveille fans—except for one thing. With the move and the construction in the north end, the scoreboard inside Kyle Field was no longer within view from Cain Park. But where there's an Aggie will, there's a way. Throughout all of the 1997 football season and even into the '98 and '99 seasons, groups of students took turns holding a dry-erase board in front of the temporary gravesite. By listening to the radio, communicating via cell phone, or going in and out of the stadium, the students updated the score inside Kyle Field for the benefit of the deceased mascots.

In the meantime, Company E-2 provided input to architects and university officials in the design phases of the new gravesite. In the summer of 2000,

Complete with her rain gear, Reveille VI participates in the march-in with Company E-2 prior to a home game at Kyle Field.
Courtesy Bo Wilson

when the stadium expansion and Zone Plaza were completed, E-2 members exhumed the coffins of five Reveilles (Rev V had died in 1999 and was buried in Cain Park) and moved them to their permanent resting place. The new gravesite, which is less than fifty feet from the original location, is the centerpiece of the plaza. The graves are surrounded by grass, highlighted by crepe myrtle trees, and covered by paving stones. At night, lights shine upon the tombstones. A small scoreboard was even installed directly in front of the graves so the Reveilles could always keep tabs on their Ags. "I took some good-natured ribbing from some of my colleagues when we put the scoreboard up outside the stadium," Groff recalled. "But to honor the tradition, it was an addition we were more than willing to make. I think the whole experience of moving the graves and moving them back, along with the publicity and outcry it generated, was an indication of how much the Reveille tradition means to so many Aggies."

It probably means more today than ever before. The university, the Corps of Cadets, Company E-2, the pedigree of the canine, and the requirements of Reveille have all undergone dramatic changes since the first Rev wandered onto campus and into the hearts of the A&M students in the early 1930s. But in many basic aspects, the tradition is still much the same. At its core, the Reveille tradition is still the prominent symbol of

Reveille VI once received a 100 on a geology test while she was attending classes with Mascot Corporal Kevin Graham, who says she was not very impressed with the perfect score. The rest of the class wondered if Rev had ruined the curve. Courtesy Jeff Bailey

Poop Deck

One reason people tend to humanize Reveille nowadays is because they do not often see her doing the things dogs normally do. While other dogs are burying bones, rolling in dirt, and scratching themselves, Reveille is most often seen in the public eye at her pristine best. Although some dogs stink, Rev usually smells better than a cadet's date. Some dogs are mangy; Reveille is elegant. And while most dogs mark their territory, Reveille is rarely seen by the public using the bathroom.

At sporting events, fans used to place bets as to where Reveille II would use the bathroom. But Rev's modern-day handlers often go to great lengths to make sure she is able to relieve herself in a more private setting. Of course, it doesn't always work out that way.

Drew Lanningham, the Mascot Corporal in 1981–82, recalls one of his most embarrassing moments at a basketball game against the University of Houston. In the heyday of the Cougars' Phi Slamma Jamma era, the Aggies and Houston met before both a packed house at G. Rollie White Coliseum and a regional television audience. At halftime, Lanningham tossed a Frisbee to Reveille IV, who entertained the crowd with her amazing ability to catch the disk on the fly. But right before the second half resumed, Lanningham decided to try one more toss.

"The referees and players started coming back, and I had time for only one more," Lanningham recalled. "The red light on the camera let me know that the TV cameras were rolling, and I released the Frisbee and she was running up and getting ready to spring up to catch it. The crowd was into it. I had everyone's attention. Everyone had been roaring real loud when she would catch it. Well this time, right as she's about to jump up, she stops right at center court and takes the biggest dump on regional TV that you've ever seen. It was so embarrassing. Nobody was my friend at that point. I had to clean it up. I had to do everything right then and there and get her off the court because the refs were already on the court with the ball. I grabbed a towel off the Aggie bench and cleaned it up and got my butt out of G. Rollie White because I couldn't show my face anymore."

so many characteristics that the university aspires to represent—friendliness, companionship, loyalty, respect, lasting bonds, and love for each other.

A&M is known far and wide for the friendly nature of its campus, as students greet each other and visitors with an array of "Howdys." Reveille's wagging tail and panting smile is an embodiment of that tradition. The Aggies are also known and admired nationally for the noise generated during athletic events by the trademark yells of the 12th Man; Rev's bellowing

During the annual picture and poster day at Kyle Field, the line to pose with Reveille is often longer than the lines to receive autographs from the A&M football players.
Courtesy Rusty Burson

bark is the perfect accompaniment. Even the humble beginnings of the original Reveille and the evolution to a pedigreed, highly respected breed seems to parallel the rise of Texas A&M's national reputation. She is a reminder of the Aggies' past, a symbol of the present, and an alluring magnet for the future, attracting toddlers to teenagers—the next generation of potential students—with a wet nose, compassionate eyes, and a sable coat.

For so many reasons, Reveille is one of the most distinctive mascots among her collegiate counterparts—just as Texas A&M is one of the most distinctive universities in the country. She is obviously not human, yet she is most definitely part of the student body, attending classes, living in the dorm, walking the campus sidewalks, and jogging with her outfit. She represents the vets—both those who practice on animals for a living and those who fought for freedom, as her five-star ranking is a constant reminder of Texas A&M's military roots. She is man's best friend on what was once an all-male campus. And while she is not perfect, she may be the perfect mascot for the Aggies because of all that she represents.

Of course, the reverence for Reveille on the A&M campus is rooted much deeper than in mere symbolism. From the original Rev to the current one, these animals have enriched the lives of countless cadets and students, boys and girls, and men and women. They have stooped to pet her, and in the process, she has uplifted them. She has continually brought out the best in those who embraced her, leaving a lasting impression in their hearts. She has made multitudes of children laugh and hundreds of grown men cry, as they have celebrated her life and mourned her passing.

Reveille VII, shown here as a puppy with Rev VI, is the largest collie mascot in the lineage of First Ladies, tipping the scales at more than seventy pounds. Courtesy Texas A&M Sports Information

Aside from the Hollywood canine stars, perhaps there has never been another series of dogs who have left such a deep and positive impression on so many as the Reveilles of Texas A&M.

"When you actually stop and think about it, it's really amazing the impact these dogs have had on thousands upon thousands of people over the years," said Dr. Joe West, who along with his wife, Carrie, was Reveille V's retirement care provider. "I was thinking about that the night Dr. Barton and her nurse came over to our house to put Rev to sleep. She was in a lot of pain, and it was obvious that it was the humane thing to do. Carrie and I and our daughter, April, had our hands on Rev and we were telling stories about her as Dr. Barton inserted the needle. Rev yawned once, closed her eyes, and we still had our hands on her when Dr.

Reveille VI poses in front of the Freedom statue at the George Bush Library on the A&M campus. Courtesy Texas A&M photographic services

Barton told us that her heart had stopped beating. It was very solemn, but it was also a very pleasant memory. She had fulfilled her role on this Earth. She had been loved and adored like few other dogs ever to walk the face of the Earth, and she had returned that love and affection many times over."

Indeed, she was something special. She was Reveille, the living, breathing, barking embodiment of not only a university, but also the power of love's effect. It wasn't her breed or her bloodlines that made her sense she was more than a dog; it was the masses of Aggies who loved her like more than a typical pet. That's what made the original Reveille so special. And in all likelihood—no matter how it continues to evolve—that's what will always make the Reveille tradition unlike any other in the university mascot domain.

Acknowledgments

SO MANY THANKS go out to all the people who helped make this book possible.

First and foremost, we cannot express how grateful we are for the incredible contributions we received from so many former Mascot Corporals, beginning with the first "unofficial" handler, Calvin Samuel Netterville. Their words, their memories, their photos are the essence of this book. Virtually every handler we interviewed was very helpful and excited about this book, but we offer a special measure of gratitude to Jerred Crumley, the Mascot Corporal in 2003–2004. Jerred didn't just share his memories and pictures; he was at our beck and call when we were on tight deadlines, delivering boxes of information and Reveille VII herself at the drop of a hat.

Special thanks also to the entire staff of the 12th Man Foundation for all of their support. Thanks to the animal lovers in the office—Toni McDowell, Reba Ragsdale, Judi Whitney, Judy Crockett, Lizett Hawkins, and Robyn Adams—for their interest and encouragement. We thank Miles Marks for allowing us the op-

portunity and providing us with the time to see it through. To Tracy Treps, Carole Dollins, Rebecca Melder, and Reagan Chessher, thanks for being around on those weekends and late summer nights and not setting off the office alarms while I was still inside. Thanks to Tricia Turner for her diligence in saving the motherboard (whatever that means) of the laptop when it died so close to deadline. Ditto to Dallas Shipp for helping us redictate some of the lost documents. And to Homer Jacobs, thanks especially for the friendship, guidance, and encouragement, as well as paving the way in the book industry. And we must single out the special contributions and sacrifices of one person in the office: Trey Wright. We may have been able to do this book without Trey's help, but it would not have been the same. We sincerely appreciate his expertise, willingness, and friendship.

We sincerely thank Lee and Joanne Phillips, Joe and Carrie West, and Charles and Diana Hall for opening up their homes first to the retired Reveilles and then to us as they shared their memories. We can only hope that we did justice to the love each of them showed to the retired Reveilles until the end.

Thanks also to men and women like Dr. Cindi Bossart, Wynn Rosser, Dr. Claudia Barton, Dr. Kay Stephens, and so many others for their background information and opinions. And speaking of background information, thanks to the entire staff of the Cushing Library for all of their researching help.

We also want to express our gratitude to the entire staff of Texas A&M University Press for choosing us to do this book and holding our hands through the process. We look forward to continuing a relationship with all of them.

Finally, thanks to our kids, Payton and Kyleigh, who basically gave up much of their 2003 summer, including a vacation, so that their parents could fulfill a dream. We love them both and pray that they will always carry with them the memories of our family dogs and share those blessings with our future grandchildren.

Index